By Phil Hall

Published by:
Larstan Publishing, Inc., 10604 Outpost Dr.,
N. Potomac MD, 20878,
240-396-0007, ext. 901
www.larstan.com

PRINTED IN THE UNITED STATES OF AMERICA

10 9 8 7 6 5 4 3 2 1

Design by Mike Gibson/Love Has No Logic Design Group (www.lovehasnologic.com)
Illustrations by Jeremy Lowther (www.jeremylowther.com)

ISBN, Print Edition 978-0-9789182-0-0

Library of Congress Control Number: 2006938965

First Edition

The New PR

An Insider's Guide to Changing the Face of Public Relations

By Phil Hall

> *"You've got to find some way of saying it without saying it."*
>
> —**Duke Ellington**

This book represents a personal culmination of more than two decades of experiences, adventures, triumphs and (on occasion) catastrophes that made up my career in the communications and media industries. It also represents a challenge for my peers working in the field and for tomorrow's leaders who will eventually reshape the depth and scope of public relations.

My first work in PR came via an internship during my freshman year at Pace University in White Plains, N.Y. I was assigned to the communications office of the Westchester Red Cross–which, conveniently, was a short walk down the street from my school. The year was 1982 and the communications environment was very different from today's. I had no Internet to rely on–in fact, I didn't even have a computer. Work was accomplished on manual typewriters, and if you wanted a duplicate copy of what you wrote, you needed to have a slice of carbon paper sandwiched between two pages (and God forbid you made a mistake in the typing!). Press releases were sent via what we now call snail mail, and our schedule demanded plenty of time be set aside for folding papers into envelopes.

That PR world is a prehistoric shadow of what we have today– and I can assure you that today's PR world will be a prehistoric shadow of what we will have two decades from now. And that's where this book comes in–the new PR is here, but too many professionals don't see the changes that are being made

Introduction and Acknowledgments

to the industry. As an insider, I can tell you that too many PR practitioners are still stuck in the past. Hopefully, this book can serve as a roadmap for the proverbial bigger and better things to come.

Creating a book is not, by any stretch, a solitary endeavor. Thus, special thanks are in order for my friends at Larstan Publishing for their wise and patient assistance in bringing this project to your hands. More thanks are in order for the many people who shared their ideas, war stories and concerns in the interviews that can be found throughout this book. They represent the best of the industry and I sincerely, hope that you will take heed of what they have to say.

Some of the material cited in this book was originally featured in (and is reprinted here) courtesy of Film Threat, Strumpette, Credit Union Business and Secondary Marketing Executive.

And, last but surely not least, a special bow of love for my family: Ma, Theo and Dewi.

Table of Contents

How Did PR Get Into Its Current State?

Foreword by Richard Berman

F

Public relations is a profession based on reputation management. It is also a profession with a serious image problem,
and it's not hard to see why. After all, any field that boasts
hit-and-run party diva Lizzie Grubman as its most recognizable practitioner could really use some good PR.

But just as the cobbler's children have no shoes, public relations executives don't seem to have the time or inclination to
improve the image of a profession that's often regarded as the
moral equivalent of raising rabbits for the cosmetics industry.

At first blush, PR's biggest problem is its reputation for obfus-
cation. The Public Relations Society of America's code of ethics
(insert snicker here) is based on the core values of advocacy,
honesty, expertise, independence, loyalty and fairness. Why,
then, does PR have a reputation for sophisticated prevari-
cation? Perhaps it's because the American people are a lot
smarter than business and political leaders think they are, and
when some spinmeister in a suit comes on television to inform
the world that seabirds actually enjoy being covered in oil,
most folks just don't buy it. As long as public relations is seen
as a tool to bury malfeasance under a web of half-truths and
distortions, the profession is going to have an unsavory reputation. It's not a coincidence that a number of anti-PR web sites
have developed avid fan bases.

But the bigger reason for the low esteem in which public relations is held is more fundamental: people simply don't know what it is. In 1998 *New York* magazine ran a cover story highlighting the new face of PR: seven winsome young women in black cocktail dresses (including a pre-scandal Lizzie Grubman) who specialized in party planning and celebrity publicity. While that kind of work certainly falls into the larger category of public relations, proclaiming them the standard bearers of the profession is the equivalent of saying that all musicians dress and act like Alice Cooper. To use a Boolean analogy, all squares are rectangles, but few rectangles are squares.

The lack of respect in which PR is held extends into corporate America. While companies usually recognize the value of corporate communications, they don't necessarily see public relations professionals as experts who should be included in core business activities. A major reason is that C-level executives rarely come out of the corporate communications ranks, and therefore they don't necessarily see the value that public relations can bring. In fact, many top executives see the mechanics of PR – including writing press releases, staffing interviews, setting up media meetings – as fairly brainless work that could easily be accomplished by a well-trained group of bonobo apes.

One of the big gripes that I have heard over the years from exasperated communications executives is that "the CEO thinks he's an expert in PR." It's unlikely that the head of a large company would claim the same level of proficiency in accounting, law, IT or other corporate functions.

One area where public relations *does* earn a degree of respect (or lack thereof, depending on how you look at it) is in the political arena. The good news is that PR pros who work for government agencies or elected officials get to be part of the inner sanctum and have a major influence on public policy. The downside is that no one trusts them. It's no accident that the most exposure that the field has gotten in the last 20 years was *Wag the Dog*, a film featuring Dustin Hoffman as a thoroughly amoral political PR operative.

In an attempt to increase the respectability of the PR profession, several attempts have been made to turn it into a "real" profession akin to law, accounting or medicine. The Universal Accreditation Board offers a program through which PR professionals can get certified with the APR (Accreditation on Public Relations) designation. It's a nice thought, but it's a voluntary effort that only a small percentage of people in the field ever pursue. And unlike the other careers where incompetence or unethical behavior can result in serious disciplinary action, there is no governing body with the power to regulate the conduct of marketing executives.

Most of the steps that the public relations profession has taken to improve its image don't address the fundamental problem, which is a lack of understanding about what PR is. That's where this book plays an invaluable role. Most of the volumes that have been written about the industry fall into three categories: university-level textbooks, the history of the profession (Stuart Ewen's excellent *PR!* comes to mind), or the practical details of creating a communications campaign.

While all of these have their place, industry veteran Phil Hall is creating a fourth category: an explanation of public relations that explores the central purpose and role of communications in the context of today's real-world business climate. In the process, he just may have inadvertently found a way to save PR from itself.

Richard Berman is CEO of VerbFactory, a public relations and marketing agency based in San Francisco.

> *"We are at a moment of great opportunity for the PR business. In a world of consumer-generated content, infinite media choices, lack of trust in traditional institutions and desire for peer-to-peer learning, we are well suited to be the communications discipline of choice. But there is a huge elephant in the room. The PR business at present lacks the credibility to take that leadership position in communications. Because we are defined by our more controversial professionals who tend to come from the political or entertainment worlds, we are characterized as spinmeisters and flacks. How can we get out of this stereotyped second-class citizen role?"*
>
> —**Richard Edelman, CEO, Edelman PR, June 5, 2006**

1

Everyone has heard of the phrase "public relations" (or "PR" for the acronym-minded), but just what does it mean? It would seem that PR means a great many things to a great many people, and that creates a pair of problems. First, the lack of a be-all/end-all definition dooms PR to endless subjective interpretations. Second, and more damaging, a lot of these interpretations are anything but positive.

As professions go, PR somehow gets clumped together with occupational pursuits that inspire various degrees of scorn and sneers: lawyers, lobbyists, politicians, insurance adjusters, tax collectors and anyone who seems to be in the business of creating more grief than goodwill.

But unlike those other professions, PR doesn't seem to have many heroes to point to with pride. There are plenty of cases where crusading lawyers or hard-hitting journalists can bring about justice or where brave elected officials can dare to stand up to the status quo. Insurance adjusters can generate a smile from those who actually profit from their processed claims.

Even lobbyists (more so of the grassroots kind versus the K Street crowd) can exact change for the better. Hey, even tax collectors can count one of their own among Christ's disciples!

But where is the popular image of the heroic publicist? Pop culture has given us a grand total of two PR professionals as iconic characters, and neither of them is truly worth admiring.

> *As professions go, PR somehow gets clumped together with occupational pursuits that inspire various degrees of scorn and sneers: lawyers, lobbyists, politicians, insurance adjusters, tax collectors and anyone who seems to be in the business of creating more grief than goodwill.*

First there was Sidney Falco, the smarmy heel in the 1957 film classic "Sweet Smell of Success." Falco was the publicist from hell: a vindictive, manipulative, dishonest, morally and intellectually bankrupt character who would say anything, do anything and hurt anyone to score an inch of ink. The fact he was played by Tony Curtis wasn't much of a consolation – having Falco played by one of the best-looking men in movies in no way diluted his malignant ooze.

Move ahead four decades and we have Samantha Jones of TV's "Sex and the City." She personified the stereotype of a New York publicist who seems to do nothing but coordinate parties and show up at special events in designer clothing. While Kim Cattrall was easy on the eyes, her character nonetheless drove home all of the lousy imagery that the general public equates with publicists.

Admittedly, there are a few other PR types who turned up via Hollywood (Jack Lemmon as the alcoholic PR executive in "Days of Wine and Roses," Billy Crystal as the wacky publicist for a quarreling Hollywood couple in "America's Sweethearts," Colin Farrell as the slimy publicist targeted by a sniper in "Phone Booth"), but those characters never truly connected with the general public's image of a PR professional. Actually, they are all fairly unsympathetic creations.

But that's just pop culture. The real world is even less helpful when it comes to locating PR role models.

In regard to visibility, the only PR professionals who appear in the public eye are the various political mouthpieces who've turned up over the years as the White House press secretary. Admittedly, they are not bona fide role model material. Just within the span of the George W. Bush presidency, we've seen the White House press briefing podiums held (with various degrees of skill and subtlety) by the likes of belligerent Ari Fleischer, bumbling Scott McClellan and ultra-smug Tony Snow. An argument could be made that some of the failure by the Bush administration in communicating its messages originated with its inefficient press spokesmen.

But in fairness, it appears that every White House has seen its share of abrasive, evasive, hostile and easy-to-exasperate press secretaries. To make matters worse, the press secretaries have sometimes made political blunders worse, thereby creating more embarrassment for their Commanders-in-Chief. For example, Richard Nixon's press secretary Ron Ziegler was negatively immortalized for brusquely dismissing the Watergate break-in as a "third-rate burglary" while George W. Bush's press secretary Tony Snow created several backlashes for surprisingly tactless statements. (He once responded to a question that was not to his liking by stating it should "die a crib death.")

The corporate world hasn't been much help either. Lizzie Grubman, who was cited in Richard Berman's foreword, has become the pinup for the worst of PR – though, in fairness, her bad cred has nothing to do with PR as a profession. For those who don't recognize her name: back in July 2001,

Grubman drove her SUV into a crowd of people outside a Long Island nightclub after being asked by security guards to move the vehicle from its inappropriate parking spot in a fire lane. She injured 16 people and fled from the scene. A plea bargain spared her from an extended prison term, and thanks to the ordeal she wound up becoming as famous as her celebrity clients – to the point of hosting her own reality TV show, "PoweR Girls," on MTV.

Even Wikipedia, the Internet's be-all/end-all/know-it-all user-edited encyclopedia, seems to have its notion of PR stuck in the muck. Witness how Wikipedia defines "publicist":

"A publicist is a person whose job is to generate and manage publicity for a public figure, especially a celebrity, or for a work such as a book or movie. Publicists usually work at large companies handling multiple clients."

Uh ... no! That is not what the ordinary publicist does. And it is certainly not what the extraordinary publicist does.

Indeed, not many people set out for a PR career during their years of impressionable youth. "I had no idea PR even existed until I met a woman through a volunteer group I was working on," recalls Colleen Coplick, CEO of Type A Public Relations in Vancouver. "We were talking about her event coordination role and, over margaritas on a patio, I discovered that she was in PR – and it sounded fascinating!"

However, Coplick began to learn more of PR as she began to study what the profession required. "What attracted me in the first place, I suppose, was a career that sounded exciting, interesting and just plain fun," she adds. "From my very narrow view at the time, I thought throwing parties for a living was glamorous. I quickly learned that PR and communications is so much more than I'd first thought – and also that I was good at it.

What attracts me to this day is the ever changing landscape I'm working in – the fact that there are external forces that I have no control over but that I need to take into account. And when it comes right down to it, I love getting media coverage. I absolutely love the adrenaline rush I get when I realize that I've landed a spot for a client in a big publication. For example, *Stuff Magazine* just ran one of my clients in their gift guide, reaching 1.9 million of our target market!"

Paul Maccabee, president of the Maccabee Group, a PR agency in Minneapolis, offers the most cogent explanation of what today's PR is all about. "At its best, public relations is the marketing discipline which facilitates effective communication between for-profit and non-profit organizations and their key audiences – customers, dealers, legislators, regulators, retailers, distributors, voters, donors and more," he says.

> *At its best, public relations is the marketing discipline which facilitates effective communication between for-profit and non-profit organizations and their key audiences – customers, dealers, legislators, regulators, retailers, distributors, voters, donors and more.*
>
> —**Paul Maccabee**

"At its best, public relations enables groups to better achieve their sales, membership, image management, fundraising and other objectives through honest persuasion in the marketplace of ideas, that clarifies the values and benefits the company/group provides to the public and its constituencies. Public relations can alert consumers to vital products and services they might never have discovered otherwise, aid groups in changing behavior (from increased seat belt use to healthier eating habits) to save lives, and help challenger brands to overcome far bigger competitors by articulating their new product benefits. That is PR at its best."

Okay, that leads to an obvious question: what's PR at its worst?

"But at its worst, public relations encompasses techniques which all too often serve as a cloak to hide corporate malfeasance, divert public attention from a business' misbehavior and fool consumers and other audiences into misperceiving an organization's true values and real-world behavior," continues Maccabee. "At its worst, public relations is exemplified by egregious corporate polluters who unveil 'green' PR campaigns that falsely paint the companies as good environmental citizens, providing cover as these 'green' companies quietly dump deadly poisons into the air, water and ground.

"At its worst, PR has been used by companies which manufactured ineffective and dangerous birth control devices to falsely convince women that their contraceptive products were effective and safe; by the U.S. tobacco industry to camouflage overwhelming evidence that their products cripple and kill their consumers and fight against the messages disseminated by health and anti-smoking advocates (with the tobacco industry aided by such PR luminaries as Ivy Lee and Ed Bernays and agencies such as Burson-Marsteller and Hill and Knowlton); by repressive foreign governments like Saudi Arabia which privately support anti-Semitic training grounds and the forces of global terrorism but use PR agencies to pretend that they are opponents of terrorism; and by the nuclear industry, to persuade the public that a destructive and unsafe technology isn't all that bad and stifle negative media coverage about nuclear dangers. All too often, PR can be used as a dark art to help a bad corporate citizen – a company which harms its community, its customers, its shareholders, its employees, and/or its neighbors – paint itself as a good corporate citizen. That is PR at its worst."

Not surprisingly, the general public rarely looks at the PR industry with undiluted admiration. It's usually quite a different emotion. And there's good reason why this is happening.

"First, there's a popularized notion that PR professionals are 'handlers' who are able to pull the wool over the eyes of the public to benefit their clients," explains Jay Stuck, president of BrandGuy Inc., Palm Beach, FL. "Second, there *really are* some PR professionals who want to pull the wool over the eyes of the public who have given the profession a negative connotation over the years. I'd like to hope much of this type of 'flacking' ended in the 1950s with the demise of Hollywood press agents, but in today's media age I am not so sure. However, the vast majority of PR professionals are highly educated and incredibly ethical. In fact, ethics is one of the major tenets promoted by our professional organizations such as the Public Relations Society of America.

"There's another reason why I think we have a negative image and I think it comes from the press. That's right, the everyday reporters with whom PR people work every day. I think that some members of the press resent PR people – they have an imaginary notion that PR folks are highly paid cop-outs that didn't earn their

> *There really are some PR professionals who want to pull the wool over the eyes of the public who have given the profession a negative connotation over the years. I'd like to hope much of this type of 'flacking' ended in the 1950s with the demise of Hollywood press agents, but in today's media age I am not so sure.*
>
> **—Jay Stuck**

chops in the pressroom and opted instead for the life of cushy corporate PR jobs. Part of it is envy and part true disdain, but some in the media don't like the fact they have to work with PR people. On some level it goes beyond just working with them; they don't like the fact they *rely* on PR people. Some, not all of the working press, resent having to need PR people to feed them stories and ideas, and I think this conflicted view ends up coming through in their work. That's why some of the stereotype about PR people is being shaped by references to them by the press. Next time you see a story published in a newspaper that references a PR person, make a mental note to see how the PR person is treated in the story or referred to. Then see if I'm right."

But what about the powers that run corporate America? It appears they often share the lack of respect for the PR function.

"I believe it is because that we are one of the least measurable practices in marketing and have done a bad job selling PR into the corporate boardroom," explains Jeremy Pepper, group manager in Weber Shandwick's San Francisco office. "We might not even have a seat at the table. Without face time, we are unable to explain the value of PR to the people who make decisions."

Suzanne O'Leary Lopez, public relations manager for Thornburg Mortgage Home Loans in Santa Fe, N.M., echoes that sentiment. "PR is complex, coverage is not as controlled as advertising or other marketing mediums, and it's more difficult to measure in terms of a marketing discipline," she notes. "As a result, most companies don't pay enough attention at the C level in terms of the importance of how PR can impact the bottom line, or commit the C-level executives to spend the 25 percent to 30 percent of their time, which is necessary to be effectual as PR ambassadors for their companies."

If we seem to be drifting into negativity, that's because the greatest challenge facing PR today is the need to redefine what PR is capable of doing. Too many people within PR are involved in a wealth of fascinating and innovative projects, yet their work is barely being recognized. Today's new PR bears no resemblance to the ill-fitting stereotypes and inappropriate behavior that has clouded public and corporate perceptions of the profession. If anything, the new PR is the most important weapon one can have in the modern marketing arsenal.

Hey, wait a minute – did I say "marketing"? Yes, I did, and before you proceed further you need to understand something that many people in the PR industry have difficulty comprehending: PR is an aspect of marketing. It is not, by any stretch of the imagination, a stand-alone practice that exists without the faintest trace of overlap with other marketing practices. In fact, the new PR benefits from borrowing strategies from its sister marketing pursuits and adapting it into its lineup of tools and weapons.

Some time ago, a self-appointed expert in all-things PR (who, ironically, never worked a day in a full-time PR environment) once stupidly sneered to me that "PR and marketing are not interchangeable expressions" (that's an exact quote). That's nonsense, of course. PR and marketing share the same goal – getting a message across to a target audience. But in today's new PR environment, reaching that goal means moving beyond the stale and restrictive limits of old-fashioned PR (the standard news release to the media route) in favor of diverse approaches and different communications avenues.

Here's an example of how PR can work effectively when it incorporates a variety of similar marketing techniques for its own needs. For Credit Union One of Oklahoma, PR has been a driving force in keeping the institution front and center with current and potential members.

In today's new PR environment, reaching that goal means moving beyond the stale and restrictive limits of old-fashioned PR (the standard news release to the media route) in favor of diverse approaches and different communications avenues.

"In the past, Credit Union One of Oklahoma has relied on promotion-based advertising to increase loan totals and membership numbers," says Ralph G. Cornelius III, marketing officer. "While the promotions have been somewhat successful, they only allowed us to coast by without any substantial growth."

During the latter part of 2006, Cornelius particularly was concerned about the credit union's marketing strategy for 2007, which involved a new push in brand name development and promotions highlighting a new branch.

"Research has showed us that PR efforts increase market awareness to build a stronger image," he continues. "For instance, our core membership is the Oklahoma Department of Human Services, with which we still have a strong relationship – yet we've had a community charter since May of 2003 and many people who are eligible to join are unaware of us. Most of them still believe that not only Credit Union One, but all credit unions are financial institutions that have strict criteria to join. We want to change this belief and increase awareness."

For Cornelius, the PR effort is aimed at a tight local audience. "In our efforts, we are mostly targeting smaller, community-based newspapers," he says. "We are using somewhat of a grassroots technique – although we do monitor media trends in the larger Oklahoma City news to look out for expanded media attention. For example, there has been a lot of buzz in the media about how high school students need to take required financial classes before graduation. It would be a great time to offer a free financial workshop open to the public and invite the media."

The Internet is also playing a role in Credit Union One's PR push. "We have made a few changes to our web site and we are working with an outside agency to rebuild the entire site," he adds. "In today's society, having a strong web site is important to how people feel about your organization."

Person-to-person communications is also crucial to the effort here. "Community relations is another new step in Credit Union One's PR efforts," explains Cornelius. "We are trying to start a team with our employees to pick an organization within our community to volunteer with. We want people to know our community is important to not only us, but them also. A growing and successful community helps us grow. During the summer of 2006, we attended four member appreciation/sponsored cookouts. At the cookouts, we teamed up with Enterprise Car Sales and usually provided hot dogs, chips, condiments, desserts, etc. The biggest cookout we did was in Muskogee, Okla., for their 70th Anniversary. The turnout was so great, we actually ran out of 500 hot dogs and had to get more."

Well, a summer cookout in the middle of Oklahoma may not seem like PR, especially if you are still hooked into the notion of celebrity publicity or political spin. But Cornelius and his credit union represent the face and soul of the new PR – an inventive, subtle and effective means of connecting with a core audience. Through a combination of event marketing, Internet marketing, grassroots marketing and the old-fashioned news release approach, the credit union has taken an inventive and proactive approach to the PR strategy.

PHIL'S INSIDER PR TIP 1 Never Buy Lunch For A Journalist

I ran my own PR agency for 10 years and never bought a single meal for a journalist. I can't say that this strategy was flawed – in the course of a decade, my clients wound up on page one of the Wall Street Journal, on "The Today Show" and "Good Morning America," and even as far afield as the BBC, Agence France Presse and (back in the fun days of the U.S.S.R.) TASS – and the party boys at the Kremlin were not ones for being wined and dined by capitalist flacks!

Let's consider some ground rules in dealing with the media. Serious and professional editors, reporters and producers feast on information that is delivered in crisp, succinct and well-cooked servings. Despite the grumblings of the media that they are barely paid enough, they are able to buy their own lunches. It is not the PR person's job to feed them. This includes all aspects of the food-for-thought exchange, from sending munchies over the holidays (my December mailbox is always overstuffed with atrocious chocolates and oversalted nuts, most of which were given away or trashed) to going the full blast with busboys tossing plates of soggy eggs at "press breakfasts."

But you may ask, what kind of journalist gets snagged with free food? This situation reminds me of a trade media character I once knew. I'll call him Ol' Lunchbucket, because he perfected the art of mooching meals in exchange for press coverage. On the surface, you might think that such an exchange contradicts our lesson. In reality, it reconfirmed it: Ol' Lunchbucket gave priority story placement to his mealtime buddies within the city where he worked.

The industry in the rest of the country (which didn't cover his lunch tab) was barely acknowledged outside of some artful rewording of press releases or rewrites of stories published in other magazines. Not surprising, Ol' Lunchbucket's publication had relatively little value for the industry he covered (because his writing placed an absurd concentration on a limited number of companies in a limited geographical sector while literally ignoring the rest of America). The man himself had his shenanigans roasted when an industry tribute of his career seemed to place a surplus of attention on his gluttony rather than his ability to break exclusive news (which, of course, is terrible PR for that guy – but that's his woe).

As a journalist, I was once wined and dined by a software entrepreneur who was eager for ink. When several weeks passed without any coverage of his software program, he kept needling me with the inquiry: "What happened to the story we discussed OVER LUNCH?" The fact that he never gave me the information I truly needed to make the story happen (exclusive client testimonials, high-res screen shots) somehow didn't sink in. He truly believed that an exchange was underway: one eggplant parmigiana lunch for 15 column inches of glowing coverage. To deal with those types of people, we'll need to drop some bromide tablets.

PR IN ACTION: A MILITARY MAKEOVER

The most effective PR is actually the PR work that attracts the least amount attention to itself. That might seem like a contradiction, but it actually makes sense. If people can stop and point and say "Aha, that's just a PR stunt!" ... well, guess what? That's the equivalent of doing a magic trick with the source of the magic in open exposure for everyone to see.

Let's look at a PR campaign where the PR strategies and mechanism were out of view to the general public. It's a case study helmed by Rick Myllenback, who served as Command Marketing Officer for the Office of Naval Intelligence (ONI), which is part of the U.S. Department of the Navy. Myllenback worked as a full-time civilian (although he is also a Navy reservist) and was also deputy director for the External Corporate Relations team that reported to the ONI's executive director. It seemed that the ONI decided it needed to rebrand its image (including its logo), which was rather unusual since it had operated under the same brand image and logo for 124 years. Myllenback explains the genesis of this PR endeavor for us in this enlightening Q&A.

Why was it determined that ONI needed a new brand image and logo after 124 years?

RICK MYLLENBACK: The field of intelligence – more specifically, military intelligence – has always been cloaked in the shadows of secrecy – for good reason. Broadcasting an intelligence organization's capabilities concerning the collection, analysis and dissemination of critically important and strategic information was never considered a priority, let alone a consideration at all. Historically, it made no sense to "market" intelligence.

The ONI, like its service intelligence counterparts, deals with extremely sensitive information, and has since its inception. There is good reason for this as Top Secret information can offer strategic insight into key elements that impact national security and provide military superiority. It gives our nation and its military forces a competitive advantage on a global scale. Good intelligence is essential to ensure successful outcomes – in virtually every circumstance, including those in business and in government.

This was no where better demonstrated than during the Cold War where the expert resource on the naval capabilities of the Soviet Union and other countries of interest resided at ONI. ONI employs world-class scientists, engineers, technicians and analysts deft at understanding numerous sea-going systems and platforms, and calculating their capabilities and intent. At that time, the audience for the information and "products" that ONI produced was extremely limited and narrow. Only a handful of senior naval officers, government officials and key strategists had a deliberate interest in the core of what was being generated by ONI and very few had a need to know – for good reason. But since the fall of the Berlin Wall and the end of the Cold War, the global defense mission shifted and ONI's role was forced to transform.

Despite the changing of the global climate – post Cold War – the great nautical wartime expertise of ONI's workforce still resided within the organization, and good naval intelligence work continued. The biggest question was how to channel that expertise in a rapidly changing world, and provide a new and growing customer base with timely, relevant and predictive maritime intelligence. At the same time, other larger intelligence organizations became far more aggressive in their recruiting efforts and set upon a strategy to be more open in their communication to a broader audience. This included the Central Intelligence

Agency (CIA), the Defense Intelligence Agency (DIA), the National Geospatial Intelligence Agency (NGA) and the National Security Agency (NSA). This was an appropriate shift in strategy and reflected a more candid approach to doing business – especially in a post-9/11 world.

Attracting and retaining key people – those with the talent, skill and aptitude for intelligence work – was a key determinant in this shift. The CIA and DIA had become very visible in their recruiting efforts, placing full-page, color advertisements in *The Washington Post* and other relevant publications and even placing limited advertisements on television. As a result of their efforts, organizations such as ONI were having more difficulty in drawing the right kinds of people, and the command actually saw some of its workforce depart for other positions – within DIA in particular. A change of strategy was essential for ONI to continue to grow its employee base.

At the same time, the Bush administration and Congress created the Office of the Director of National Intelligence to largely oversee the efforts and activities of the U.S. intelligence community and provide guidance and direction in its function and output. This represented a paradigm shift for all U.S. based intelligence organizations. For many of the 16 or so intelligence organizations that were to come under the purview of the Director of National Intelligence, their core missions remained largely the same. But a shift in the need and awareness for other types of intelligence work rapidly emerged – especially as it related to homeland security and homeland defense. The potential impact to ONI was profound. Suddenly, the need for maritime intelligence on a global basis became a huge priority. Tracking the status of hundreds of thousands of strategic seagoing vessels, including tankers, container ships, merchant ships, warships and many other sea-based craft, all at the same time, became of great national interest. There was no better an organization to handle this complex and intense task. ONI was ready and ideally situated.

It was also recognized that, while a great deal of information that passed through the halls of the National Maritime Intelligence Center (NMIC), headquarters for ONI, was of a highly classified nature, a great deal was unclassified, including key missions in support of homeland security. This gave the leadership the impetus to be more open in its communication to key constituencies and targeted audiences – without divulging anything classified.

With the shift in the openness of the larger intelligence organizations; combined with a rapidly changing environment; a fight for limited resources – primarily money and people; and a shift in the mission and new priorities; organizations such as ONI would be forced to seize the opportunity or to reject it. Overcoming the natural instinct to remain secretive and secure, ONI, under its visionary and courageous leaders, sought change and the chance to have an impact in new and different ways.

This called for a change in the way ONI did business, both in the way it positioned itself in the community and in the way it communicated information about the organization. The focus was now directed to proactively generate greater visibility and have more of a posture within the national intelligence community – within DIA and the Department of Defense, within the Department of Homeland Security and even on Capitol Hill, for precious resources and to secure a leading and relevant role in the ever changing wartime environment. For more than 100 years, ONI has been recognized as the expert resource for global maritime intelligence, now it was time to reinforce and solidify that position on a broader stage.

ONI wasn't alone in understanding the new situation requiring a more business-like approach, to include marketing as a key element. NGA, for instance, repositioned itself by changing its name and updating its identity. While still providing key mapping and imagery intelligence information, it changed its name from a somewhat antiquated National Imagery and Mapping Agency (NIMA) to a more robust National Geospatial-Intelligence Agency. It adopted NGA as its moniker and completely changed its seal from the traditional, flat, two-dimensional government seal (such as the Seal of the President of the United States) to a modern, colorful, three-dimensional image of the earth and space. The seal also became its logo.

At the same time, ONI's commanding officer, executive director and executive leadership team felt it was time to move ONI into a more visible position and become more proactive in its external communications. It also made a priority of getting better connected with its customers and external audiences. In doing so, ONI's leadership created a new management function, that of Command Marketing, reporting to the director of External Corporate Relations. The charter of the Command Marketing Officer was to focus on getting closer to its customers and generating more visibility with key external constituents.

Upon accepting that position, the External Corporate Relations team set about generating a marketing plan designed to methodically move ONI to become more customer-focused, market-oriented and modern in its image. Taking inspiration from the groundbreaking work done at NGA, we knew the value of the three letter moniker – ala FBI, CIA, DIA, NSA. After all, NGA gave up its widely accepted "NIMA" and compressed the words Geospatial with Intelligence into a hyphenated word, and came up with NGA. We knew that there was a great deal of equity in the letters "ONI" and it didn't require re-inventing. At one time, during World War II, ONI was as well known as the FBI. Everyone within the intelligence community and certainly all U.S. Navy personnel knew about ONI. With its century-old heritage and a great legacy of successes, ONI was prime for re-branding, polishing and modernizing, and being re-introduced to a broader external audience. All that was needed was to highlight ONI in a more tangible manner which required a new approach and a new look. This was the impetus in the creation of the ONI logo, along with a strategic branding and identity campaign.

In creating a new logo for ONI, we set about the challenge of seeking something very different and distinctive while keeping rooted in its great heritage and connection to the U.S. Navy. We felt that the command needed to go beyond updating its official seal, as NGA did, and generate a visible image that differentiated it from the multitude of seals already in place. This didn't mean abandoning the seal, just creating a logo that differentiated ONI from the rest. The seal would continue to be used for official correspondence and other more formal functions. The logo would be used on everything else, including all of ONI's products, publications, reports and presentations. It would be used on posters, business cards, tradeshow displays, marketing materials, folders, its web site, multimedia productions and everywhere else the logo could appear. It became the standard visual representation of and for the command.

In designing the new logo we needed to ensure that it embodied the essence and spirit of ONI yet differentiated it from the standard official seal. The new ONI logo visually depicts key elements of the organization. This includes the bold, embossed, heavy metal look of the lettering, representing ONI's durability and toughness ("Built Ford Tough"), endurance and stability. The metallic look also represents ONI's connection to the U.S. Navy – haze, gray and underway. The italicized font represents accelerating motion – the forward thinking nature of the organization. The embossed, 3-D look symbolizes the depth and diverse nature of the ONI workforce along with the deep technical knowledge, expertise and character of ONI. The blue water symbolizes the oceans of the world and ONI's global role in keeping the sea-lanes open and its fleet safe – ready to respond to any crisis at any moment, anywhere in the world. The red line represents the Marine Intelligence component of ONI and the partnership the two organizations share. It also represents the laser-like approach to everything the command does. The words "Office of Naval Intelligence" deliver on the letters "ONI" and underscore the confidence and pride in the organization and its rich heritage.

We developed an *ONI Standards Guide* book to make sure the logo and seal were used in the proper manner and not artistically defaced or used in any rogue fashion, and became the "logo cops," essentially the keepers of the message and defenders of the brand.

We also needed to make sure that the logo was well accepted and embraced by the workforce – ONI's greatest resource and its best source for external communication.

Well, that was quite an answer! In dealing with a government agency, what were the levels of command that you needed to go through before your design was officially approved?

RICK MYLLENBACK: Interestingly enough, the concept of a logo was so new to the organization that it was amazingly uncomplicated to get approved from command leadership. Few of the military leaders knew what to do with it initially, so there was little opposition from the start. The most difficult part was creating a logo that properly represented the organization. Once the logo was created and fine-tuned, people liked it. The next step was to explain the difference between a seal, a logo and an emblem, and how each should be used. In the past, the seal was all that was used. It represented the identity for the command. With a new marketing approach, we were able to convince the leadership and the workforce that the identity of the command was O-N-I, and that ONI was to be highlighted at every opportunity.

Once we embarked on the creation of the logo, we presented various concepts to small teams and informal groups to get their feedback. My boss, Jim Boyd, the director of External Corporate Relations, and a 27-year veteran of ONI, had a large say in which early logo concepts were better than others, and why. Gradually, three concepts emerged which were then whittled down to one which was worked and re-worked until it met our standards. Large credit goes to Booz Allen Hamilton and its graphics team for its assistance, because ONI did not have that graphics-intense capability in-house. Once the final concept was completed and a prototype logo generated, it was reviewed by the special Command Marketing Council we had formed. The Command Marketing Council (composed of members from all of the directorates within ONI and select representation from external sources including the Naval Intelligence Professionals organization) provided valuable input which led to the creation of the final version. At the same time we were getting feedback from the Command Marketing Council, we were getting buy-in from the command leadership by briefing them on the status of the project and gaining its insight and approval.

By the time we presented the logo concept to the Executive Leadership Team (ELT) – the equivalent of a board of directors for ONI – everyone had seen it, had a say in it and had largely bought into the concept. There was little resistance with the adoption of the logo at that point. The only opposition came from a few whose mindset was still stuck in the 1980s Cold War era, and who saw little value in the need to "market" ONI.

Once the logo was approved by the ELT, it was officially approved by the Commanding Officer in the form of an official memo and adopted by the command. The logo design and description was also forwarded to ONI's Judge Advocate General (JAG) Officer who subsequently submitted it for legal approval and the pursuit of a trademark. This was done in much the same way as the Air Force with the re-design of their logo. After that, it was widely accepted by the command and its affiliates, including the Reserve components, and became widely recognized by those familiar with ONI – especially the customer base.

Can you please provide more detail regarding the internal communications campaign that initiated employee involvement and buy-in? Which employees in particular were targeted, and what did this campaign consist of?

RICK MYLLENBACK: Getting internal buy-in and acceptance from the workforce-at-large presented the greatest challenge in establishing the new ONI logo. The general mindset – and actual culture – of ONI was one of cloak-and-dagger secrecy, stealth and a quiet, brush-off denial of the existence of the organization. There was a general paranoia about saying anything to anyone about ONI and its role within the intelligence community and in its activities in supporting the fleet. But there was also a tremendous amount of pride on the part of each person and the role they play in support of ONI's mission and in having a hand in a greater good – supporting freedom and democracy around the world. We wanted to harness the pride of the organization and leverage that energy to ONI's benefit, to increase its stature within its various communities. We also wanted to better utilize ONI's employees as the command's key spokespeople – especially for recruiting and retention purposes.

Overcoming the Cold War mentality of the workforce would be our greatest obstacle and continues to be an issue even today. The concept of marketing was so foreign to the organization that it required tireless outreach and interaction with ONI employees every day to explain the concept, purpose and existence of marketing before they would understand it. Most supported the concept that ONI needed to have a better understanding of its customers and most agreed that ONI needed to become more visible in an increasingly competitive "marketplace." They had a difficult time with the notion that they were allowed to talk more freely about ONI and its value to national security – without revealing anything classified. Some completely embraced the idea and many were encouraged to try. But a couple of old, curmudgeon Cold Warriors remained, who were opposed to change and resisted disrupting the status quo. It was with the direct endorsement of the three commanding officers (Capt. Tom Bortmes, Rear Admiral Tony Cothron and Capt. Alex Butterfield) and two executive directors (Ms. Claudia Erland and Mr. Greg Spencer) under whom we worked over the course of more than two years, who took personal interest in seeing our program succeed and supported our every effort.

Generating buy-in from the workforce required a new and unique set of tactics for the command. With the blessing of the command leadership, we initiated a command-wide contest to create a new overall tagline. Where none had existed before, the External Corporate Relations team created one as a placeholder: "Excellence in Global Maritime Knowledge." This was designed to get the workforce thinking about a one-line descriptor for the organization. Then we opened it up for employee input. Over the course of three weeks, with the commanding officer's blessing, we managed an employee-wide tagline contest that drew more than 300 individual inputs! Many of the suggestions were quite good. The External

Corporate Relations team reviewed all 300 or so entries and pared it down to the top 30. The top 30 were reviewed by the Command Marketing Council and 10 were given to the ELT, upon which three were selected and presented to the Commanding Officer. His pick: "ONI: Timely – Relevant – Predictive." This was a good descriptor for a great organization and was well accepted by the workforce. A special shirt with the ONI logo was presented to the person with the winning submission. This widespread contest generated a great buzz within the entire command and went a long way in softening the hard-line perception about marketing. The tagline is still used to this day, along with the logo in all marketing materials produced by ONI.

Additionally, the quarterly ONI internal newsletter, *The Intelligencer*, also was used to communicate information about the logo and the branding and identity of ONI. The publication schedule for *The Intelligencer* was shifted from quarterly to monthly and distributed online as well as in hard copy to ensure more widespread coverage.

Please detail the All-Hands Town Hall meeting that introduced the new logo and campaign.

RICK MYLLENBACK: To top off all internal activities, a special All-Hands "town hall" style meeting was called by the commanding officer at which time we were allowed to address the command in person and unveil the new logo and provide commentary. With a live audience of more than 400 people – standing room only in the main NMIC auditorium – and the ability to address the rest via internal video, I was able to reach the nearly 1,200 employees of ONI simultaneously. The remaining 1,300 remote employees were able to view the video via the Intranet at a later date and time via archived format.

For the All-Hands meeting, we created a brief PowerPoint deck that provided a quick overview of our marketing programs and their purpose and set the stage for the unveiling of the new logo. During the presentation, we used one slide that placed the ONI seal on the same slide as many of the other government seals, suggesting that the ONI seal was "one among many" and got lost among the myriad. What was needed, I explained, was something distinctive that set ONI apart from the rest. That is when we revealed the new ONI logo. I discussed the purpose behind its creation and what it represented. I used the Air Force as an example of updating its "star and wing" logo to be more modern and representative of the new Air Force. I also used a slide to show many of the more recognizable corporate logos and how they are impactful and memorable. At the conclusion of the presentation, I was given a round of applause from the audience – a rarity during All-Hands meetings. The commanding officer at the time, Rear Admiral Tony Cothron, proceeded to provide a verbal endorsement saying that he was behind the branding and identity effort, supported and approved of the new logo, and asked that everyone begin to use it at all times.

I am proud of what we were able to accomplish in a short amount of time – starting from scratch – with an organization that had never done any form of marketing ever before in 124 years. What we created is a distinctive, impactful logo and a brand and identity that is truly representative of ONI, the organization and all within it. It packages the heritage of ONI with a modern, solid look conveying strength, character and stability. We did this primarily with internal ONI graphics and creative services resources, along with the use of Booz Allen Hamilton's Creative Media Solutions Group, and the design services of Laurel Marketing Design (LMD) of Laurel, Md. Remarkably, we were granted a budget of merely $50,000 to use for external resources, of which only a fraction was used to create the logo itself.

POINTS TO REMEMBER

PR needs better PR. Oddly, this is an industry that does a great job in publicizing everything ... except itself. From an external image dilemma, PR needs more work in defining its strengths and opportunities with the general public.

To reiterate something said earlier by Jay Stuck: "There's a popularized notion that PR professionals are 'handlers' who are able to pull the wool over the eyes of the public to benefit their clients. Of course, there *really are* some PR professionals who want to pull the wool of the eyes of the public who have given the profession a negative connotation over the years. I'd like to hope much of this type of 'flacking' ended in the 1950s with the demise of Hollywood press agents, but in today's media age I am not so sure. However, the vast majority of PR professionals are highly educated and incredibly ethical. In fact, ethics is one of the major tenets promoted by our professional organizations such as the Public Relations Society of America."

Within the business world, PR also needs to redefine its importance in the overall marketing environment. "Accurate and meaningful measurement of PR success is, in my mind, the greatest challenge," says Nate Towne, president of Xanadu Communications in Madison, Wisc. "It is the return on investment that drives the spending decisions of executive bean counters. It's important to demonstrate that PR can be more cost-effective and influential than other aspects of the marketing mix (such as advertising) in order to keep PR a viable and pivotal part of the integrated marketing plan."

Where Did PR Come From and Where is it Going?

> *"Publicity is the life of this culture – in so far as without publicity capitalism could not survive – and at the same time publicity is its dream."*
>
> —**John Berger, Ways of Seeing (1980)**

2

It would be nice to say that PR is the world's oldest profession, but another vocation got there first. Yet PR would probably have a good chance of laying claim for being the second oldest profession, because mankind has been promoting itself vigorously ever since it jettisoned the caveman shtick and embraced the niceties of civilization.

Seriously! Consider the cave paintings in Lascaux, which can be dated back to 25,000 B.C. (give or take a year). Created by the Paleolithic forerunners of today's French, the Lascaux's art was not painted for sake of stylish interior decoration (that came much later in French culture). Rather, the paintings were meant to document the lives – and in at least one case, a death – relating to a tribe of cave-dwelling hunters. In creating this extraordinary record, the Lascaux tribe provided the first recorded instance of self-promotion.

American PR is traced back to the American Revolution. This may sound like a fairly loopy statement, but the Revolution was actually the first time in the history of civilization that publicity stunts and media manipulation were used to overthrow one government in favor of a new leadership.

Today's PR industry in the United States actually has its roots in history. In order to understand where public relations stands today and where it is heading in the future, it is important to determine how it evolved into the industry we have today.

American PR is traced back to the American Revolution. This may sound like a fairly loopy statement, but the revolution was actually the first time in the history of civilization that publicity stunts and media manipulation were used to overthrow one government in favor of a new leadership.

It all began rather badly on March 5, 1770, with what became known as the "Boston Massacre." The roots of the event were anything but stirring: a wigmaker's teenaged apprentice asked a British officer for payment on an overdue barber's bill. A British sentry responded to this request by clubbing the youth on the head. The young man ran off and came back later with a crowd of angry Bostonians, who began throwing snowballs and garbage at the sentry and his comrades. The soldiers increased their numbers and the locals were soon joined by other angry civilians. As with any hostile standoff between a crowd of civilians and a crowd of armed and angry soldiers, it didn't end very well for the civilians: five men died and six were wounded when the soldiers opened fire on the crowd.

However, this incident was used by the pro-independence factions as a rallying cry for the separation of the colonies from Great Britain (which was rather peculiar, because it had nothing to do with the socio-economic conditions that fueled the talk of separatism). The colonists dubbed the event the "Boston Massacre" – whether you could actually call it a massacre is open to debate, considering the relatively small number of people shot in an angry crowd that reportedly grew into the hundreds.

But the pro-independence forces used this as their PR tool. Artist Henry Pelham and engraver Paul Revere (yes, the Midnight Ride guy) created and distributed prints of the event that took considerable liberties on what actually happened. In these distorted recreations, Capt. Thomas Preston, the Officer of the Day, is shown giving the pre-meditated order to fire on the crowd – in reality, a private named Hugh Montgomery, who was felled by a chunk of ice thrown by the mob, was the first to shoot off his weapon and yell "Fire!"

Furthermore, many of the prints that circulated after the event did not make mention of Crispus Attucks, an African-American who was one of the five men killed in the gunfire. Having a black martyr did not help the cause of the pro-independence movement, so he was omitted from the re-creation. Ironically, Attucks would be re-inserted into the story of the Boston Massacre decades later by abolitionists who used him as an example of heroism and bravery among the African-American population. That bit of historical PR ensured Attucks would be the only name most people recognize among the slain (for the record, the other four men who were killed were Samuel Gray, James Caldwell, Samuel Maverick and Patrick Carr).

Let's stay in Boston but fast-forward three years. At this time, the British East India Company had a monopoly on the import of Chinese tea to the colonies without having to pay taxes, thus undercutting the prices offered by tax-paying merchants. The problems with this situation were (pardon the pun) brewing to December 16, 1773. That evening, about 150 white Boston men dressed up like Mohawk Indians boarded three British ships in Boston Harbor and tossed the contents of 342 crates of tea into the water. And, thus, America's first publicity stunt took place with the Boston Tea Party.

In retrospect, this action failed to achieve any of its goals (and no one was fooled by the Indian disguises – it was fairly obvious which pro-independence leaders were behind the action). Yet the brazen nature of the stunt and the speed with which the news spread was the best PR the anti-British factions could ever hope to achieve.

Let's fast-forward another three years, stopping at January 10, 1776. On this day, the first edition of the monograph "Common Sense" was published. Thomas Paine wrote that tract, but due to its incendiary nature he chose not to identify his authorship. It didn't matter. At a time when the colonies had a population of four million, "Common Sense" sold 120,000 copies in its first printing, making it second to the Bible as the most popular publication of its time. It also inspired a wave of counter-attack monographs, most notably James Chalmers' "Plain Truth" (thus pioneering the notion of PR counterattacks).

Subsequent editions of "Common Sense" and Paine's series of pamphlets called "The Crisis" helped to explain, with eloquence and cogent focus, the purpose of the revolt against British rule. For the first time, a political movement used its own media to spread the word on its goals and actions.

Even in post-Revolution America, PR existed solely as a political communications tool. This made sense because there was no need for corporate PR, let alone lifestyle PR (those pursuits came later – be patient and we'll get to them in due time).

In the late 18th and early 19th centuries, the use of the media to influence popular opinion took two distinctive approaches. There was either the positive strategy designed to build a consensus of support for particular issues via intellectual punditry (most notably in the series of articles known collectively as The Federalist Papers), and there was the negative strategy to tear down prominent political figures (the 1802 news stories outing President Thomas Jefferson's affair with his black slave Sally Hemings). It should be noted that the media of that period was anything but objective, and too often the publishers would happily promote whatever agenda suited them best, regardless of its effects on the delivery of news.

As the 19th century progressed, political PR became more sophisticated. In 1820, President Andrew Jackson named Amos Kendall as his press secretary, offering the first gatekeeper between the media and the Oval Office. In 1840, the Whig Party was able to secure the White House for the first time during the presidential election thanks to the aggressive campaign promotions surrounding candidate William Henry Harrison (the military hero from the Battle of Tippecanoe) and his running mate John Tyler (a fairly nondescript politician). The "Tippencanoe and Tyler, Too" campaign slogan was a catchy alliteration that stuck with voters, as did the stunt of a giant decorated ball with campaign promises that was rolled through cities in political parades. That stunt is still with us: it is the origin of the expression "keep the ball rolling."

Around this time, PR was shown to have a value beyond politics. In 1842, British writer Charles Dickens did his first public reading tour of the United States. Dickens' novels were hugely successful on this side of the Atlantic, and the visit of the British writer virtually invented the genre of literary PR. Dickens' tour also created a PR brouhaha: it resulted in the harsh reception on this side of the Atlantic to his "American Notes," a devastating critique of the nation's less sophisticated practices (including slavery, the mistreatment of those incarcerated in penitentiaries and mental asylums, the lifestyles of uneducated rural communities and the absence of copyright protections).

Whatever success Dickens enjoyed in his American tour was overshadowed by the PR mania generated in 1850. During that year, showman P.T. Barnum brought the Swedish soprano Jenny Lind to the United States for a concert tour. Barnum went overboard in stirring up a media frenzy for the singer, who became the first celebrity superstar in American culture. Her impact was so strong that her concert in Washington, D.C., saw the members of Congress and the Supreme Court putting their official business on hold to be a part of her audience.

Barnum also took an unprecedented PR step in offering Jenny Lind as a celebrity endorser. A variety of products bearing her name and image began to flood the marketplace, and some enterprising people decided to piggyback on this by using Jenny Lind's name without her permission – most notably a California town that rechristened itself as Jenny Lind (which is odd, as she never made it to California during her American tour and the people living there probably never heard her voice).

Barnum was no stranger to celebrity-building PR campaigns – he was responsible for turning sideshow attractions such as the conjoined siblings Chang and Eng Bunker (the original "Siamese Twins") and the midget Gen. Tom Thumb into household names. But Jenny Lind's fame came from personality and talent, not physical deformity, which redefined how American society viewed creative artists.

As the 19th century continued, America would become awash with a seemingly endless number of attention-seeking individuals who sought fame and fortune by exhibiting (or perhaps exploiting) their personality and talent. Some self-promoters were not lacking in star value: Dr. Mary E. Walker, the only woman to win the Medal of Honor during the Civil War, made a lucrative postwar career out of public speaking tours while the Irish wit Oscar Wilde created a sensation in his 1882 American tour (which was sponsored by the producer Richard D'Oly Carte, who followed Wilde with the American tour of the Gilbert and Sullivan operetta "Patience," which had its own Wilde-like character in the musical mix).

Yet many of these brazen exhibitionists, it seemed, had more personality than talent. The Wild West unleashed a surplus number of these characters, most notably Buffalo Bill Cody, who reinvented the popular image of the frontier experience with his raucous touring shows of brave cowboys and "savage Indians." This marked the first time in the United States that popular entertainment reconfigured public perceptions of history (it was great PR for the cowboys, but not so great for the Indians). Then there was the case of Martha Canary, a.k.a. Calamity Jane. Her exact talents were always on the hazy side, and most of her fame stemmed from a series of dime novels featuring a "Calamity Jane" superhero-type character (a far cry from the raucous, alcoholic Canary). Still, she got plenty of mileage from being famous, and her self-promoting talents would make Paris Hilton seem like a rank amateur.

In 1874, a national touring network of entertainment, educational and spiritual presentations called the Chautauqua Circuit was established to bring a variety of messages and messengers to wider audiences. It was organized by the Rev. John H. Vincent (a Methodist minister) and businessman Lewis Miller at the Chautauqua Lake campsite in upstate New York. Initially it was designed to train Sunday school teachers via an outdoor summer school environment (don't ask why they opted to go outdoors rather than offer lessons in the traditional indoors manner). The adult summer camp format caught on and Chautauqua-like gatherings soon became commonplace throughout North America; the name Chautauqua stuck with this sector, despite the obvious fact it was difficult to spell and pronounce. While many of these assemblies focused on musical entertainment and spiritual lectures, others were used to spread political and social reform messages (the Populist Party candidates of the late 19th century were especially active here). The latter consideration was especially crucial because many of the Chautauqua gatherings took place in rural areas where there was limited or no mass media – thus, these presentations were truly major events.

Mass media killed the Chautauqua Circuit – the wild popularity of motion pictures and radio brought the world to once-distant audiences, who preferred the manufactured entertainment to live presentations.

The latter part of the 19th century saw more permanent fixtures of PR take root. In the 1880s, New York was in the center of the PR spotlight with two impromptu stunts that became part of the publicity lexicon regarding the use of a city as a PR venue. In 1883, concerns over the stability of the newly constructed Brooklyn Bridge were answered at the last minute when P.T. Barnum returned to the spotlight with a parade of circus elephants walking across the structure. Three years later, the opening of the Statue of Liberty was met with an unexpected festivity: the first ticker-tape parade. This exuberant (if somewhat messy) celebration became a staple of public celebrations for the length of the 20th century.

The last years of the 19th century incorporated telephonic communications into the PR bag of tricks. In 1896, presidential candidate William McKinley made the first telephone outreach calls as part of his campaign. The telephonic touch helped McKinley win headlines and, more important, win the election – and that tactic is still with us.

In 1896, presidential candidate William McKinley made the first telephone outreach calls as part of his campaign. The telephonic touch helped McKinley win headlines and, more important, win the election – and that tactic is still with us.

By the 20th century, PR began to permeate the corporate world. It actually came at the right time, as the muckraking popular media and headline-grabbing politicians were rallying against dubious business practices by America's major corporate powers and their abuses (genuine and perceived) against the basic tenets of decency and fair play. These corporate powers needed to put a better face on their capitalist activities and not allow their image to be molded by hostile outside forces.

To answer that call, a new type of company was created that allowed the corporate world to have their image molded by friendly outside forces. In 1900, The Publicity Bureau was opened as America's first PR agency in Boston, and it aimed at helping to redefine public perception of its corporate client list. Other agencies began to spring up, but even here a danger existed that too much PR would be misconstrued as spin and hype. (Sounds familiar, yes?)

In 1906, a man named Ivy Lee (who co-founded the pioneering PR agency Parker and Lee) published "Declarations of Principles." This manifesto was remarkable in its linkage of the PR profession with the concept of ethics and responsibilities. Ironically, Lee didn't practice what he preached: in 1914 he was hired by Standard Oil after a bloody Colorado coal mining uprising known as the Ludlow Massacre (the company needed to clean up its image in the face of the gruesome event). At the time of his death in 1934, Lee was under Congressional investigation concerning his activities on behalf of IG Farben, a Nazi corporation.

While Lee's manifesto was aimed at his PR peers, other publications took the PR message to a wider audience. Edward Bernays published *Crystallizing Public Opinion* in 1923 and "Propaganda" in 1928, and these texts offered an introduction to PR theories and practices that are still in use today (the latter book found its title integrated into the everyday vernacular). Bernays, a nephew of Sigmund Freud, was no slouch as a publicist – his corporate client list included CBS, Procter & Gamble and General Electric, and he even went so far as to orchestrate 1929 as a national celebration of the 50th anniversary of Thomas Edison's invention of the light bulb (complete with the issuance of a U.S. commemorative postage stamp of the event, a philatelic PR first).

If Bernays had a rival for popularity within the PR sphere, it would've been Arthur W. Page. In 1927, Page was named vice president of public relations for AT&T. That appointment, made by AT&T CEO Walter Gifford, was the first time an internal communications professional was brought into the upper echelons of corporate power to become personally involved in guiding a company's business strategies. Page's influence stretched beyond the AT&T boardroom: he authored a guide to PR protocol that became known as the Page Principles. The Arthur W. Page Society, a trade association that credits itself with maintaining high standards in today's industry, is named in his honor.

While corporate America was polishing the art of PR, the entertainment industry was stretching PR to new extremes. The nascent motion pictures industry relied heavily on PR to attract audiences to the medium, and a heavy emphasis was placed on its new stars. In 1910, producer Carl Laemmle created a stunt that spread the rumor of the death of his biggest star, Florence Lawrence, in a New York streetcar accident. Laemmle had Lawrence make a personal appearance in St. Louis to show she was still alive. Lawrence was also notable as the first movie star (or to be specific, the first performer to be clearly identified in the promotional aspects of a movie), and her fame rested solely on the publicity that Laemmle's company generated on her behalf. Lawrence also represents the darker side of PR's ephemeral nature: in 1915, she was burned in a studio fire. She returned to work the following year, but collapsed after completing a film and was paralyzed. Her health recovered, but she was off-screen until 1921 and was unable to gain anything but small roles. Bankrupted in the Great Depression and plagued with poor health, she committed suicide in 1938 by eating ant paste. She was buried in an unmarked grave in Hollywood Cemetery – an ironic end to a career that briefly soared via PR's outreach.

In 1915, the first "invented" movie star hit the screens when a sweet young girl from Ohio named Theodosia Goodman was rechristened as the sultry vamp Theda Bara. Publicity about the movie industry quickly dominated the arts and culture media in the early part of the 20th century, to the point that scandals relating to film performers (including murder charges against Roscoe "Fatty" Arbuckle and the drug-related death of leading man Wallace Reid) created a public revulsion against the perceived excesses of the movie world (that revulsion, of course, didn't last very long).

Ah, but what about political PR? The federal government, which was never the savviest in regard to proactive PR, caught up with the private sector in the first part of the 20th century. World War I saw President Woodrow Wilson's administration take an uncommonly imaginative approach to the subject in 1917 when the Committee on Public Information was created, marking the first time the government coordinated wartime communications and propaganda through a central point of command. Calvin Coolidge was the first president to reach out to the public via radio. He even agreed to appear in an experimental sound film reel, and he also participated in various publicity-oriented photo opportunities (including the notorious photograph where he donned an Indian war bonnet). Coolidge's camera time was not in vain: the so-called White House "photo ops" are still with us.

Yet it was during the presidency of Franklin D. Roosevelt that Washington's PR machinery was truly perfected. Roosevelt was crippled from polio, yet through a pre-arranged agreement between the White House and the press corps there were to be no photographs or newsreels of the president struggling to walk. This was a brilliant PR coup, as Roosevelt's ebullient personality was clearly at odds with the physical challenges of living with polio. (In fact, only one unauthorized piece of newsreel footage showing Roosevelt walking with heavy metal braces on his legs is known to exist – and it was never seen during his lifetime.)

Roosevelt's celebrated Fireside Chats, which began in 1933, were radio broadcasts that allowed the president to completely bypass the media and speak directly to the American public – thus allowing him to have full control over the message. Presidential addresses to the nation, first on radio and then on television, became commonplace with all successive administrations. During World War II, Roosevelt reached out to Hollywood via the Office of War Information, a federal agency designed to build public support for America's military efforts. The top film talents of the day (including Frank Capra, John Huston and William Wyler) were recruited to craft propagandistic documentaries to explain why the country went to war and to detail the challenges of battle.

Another federal endeavor, the War Advertising Council, was created under Roosevelt's guidance in 1942 to produce public service posters and advertisements (most notably the Rosie the Riveter image). After the war, it was rechristened as The Advertising Council and became the central clearinghouse for public service announcements on behalf of federal agencies and a select number of nonprofits with some degree of government connections (including the American Red Cross).

Postwar American saw PR evolve with even greater focus and sophistication. The industry saw the creation of the Public Relations Society of America in 1948 and the Foundation for Public Relations Research and Education (later renamed the

Institute for Public Relations) in 1956. Federal PR efforts to fight Communism in the Cold War environment were aided by Radio Free Europe in 1949, the United States Information Agency in 1953 and the Peace Corps in 1961.

Even foreign entities and leaders used effective PR strategies to communicate directly with the American public. The year 1951 saw the debut of the sale of State of Israel Bonds in the U.S., which has become one of the most effective PR tool for securing American financial support of the Israeli government. The United Nations tapped Danny Kaye in 1954 as its first UNICEF Goodwill Ambassador, with the goal of calling attention to issues and crises facing children in the developing world. Even Fidel Castro scored PR points in 1960 when he used his guest residency at Harlem's Hotel Theresa as a platform to call attention to America's racial problems.

Political theater (for lack of a better expression) was the most effective PR tool of the 1960s and 1970s. The Civil Rights Movement and the Women's Lib Movement relied heavily on promoting their respective agendas through mass demonstrations. Derided by the detractors of their time as noisy publicity stunts, these activities have since become defined as turning points in America's social history – albeit with legend washing over the truth (Martin Luther King Jr. was not the sole speaker in the 1963 March on Washington, and the women who staged the protest outside the 1968 Miss America pageant did not burn their bras on the Atlantic City Boardwalk).

Corporate PR rose to the occasion during the latter part of the 20th century. One of the most significant PR milestones was Johnson & Johnson's reaction to the news of tampering with its Extra Strength Tylenol brand in the Chicago area. Seven people died after swallowing capsules that were laced with cyanide. Johnson & Johnson took the lead on the matter, voluntarily withdrawing all Tylenol products on the market (some 31 million bottles). The company's vigorous handling of the crisis was rewarded when the product was reintroduced in tamper-proof packaging (a first for over-the-counter medicine) – the Tylenol brand rebounded to become the most popular retail analgesic.

The 20th century PR odyssey closed in on cyberspace. Many people came to the online world thanks to a nifty PR stunt that America Online started in 1993: the distribution of free software disks that enabled people to go Net surfing via AOL.

The year 1993 also saw the birth (perhaps accidentally) of the Internet's capacity of being able to spread unique information: the insistence that Pink Floyd's classic album "Dark Side of the Moon" could be lined up for a brilliant synchronization with the movie "The Wizard of Oz." (Yes, that's how the online rumor mill began!)

In 1996, a young lady named Jennifer Ringley set up a newfangled device called a webcam at her computer. Creating a web site she called JenniCam, Ringley allowed the growing Net community to view her 24/7. She may not have been the first person to achieve self-promotion in such a manner, but the word-of-mouth on JenniCam (coupled with the promise of catching the lovely young lady in various states of undress) helped solidify the Net as a source for PR-worthy buzz.

In 1999, Net-based PR was firmly established when the web site for a low-budget horror film literally scared the life out of unsuspecting people who came to it. The film, of course, was "The Blair Witch Project" (the web site, incredibly, is still online).

THE VIEW FROM TODAY

So where do we find the PR world today? Several key issues and concerns shape how PR functions, both as its own industry and as a major factor within the daily bump and grind of the national economy and culture.

Spin City, Part One

If many people have a negative perception of PR, it could easily be because of the "spin" element that goes with it. There have been two key factors driving the spin element: the federal government and the corporate sector. Let's start in Washington.

History will remember George W. Bush's administration for a great many things, but from a PR perspective the Bush years will be recalled as a time when public affairs communications went into overdrive – often with disastrous results. Bush was not the first president to use PR with reckless aggression, but he stands out for overstepping the lines between public affairs communications and the blatant commandeering of the media.

In 2006, the Government Accountability Office reported that the Bush White House spent $197 million on 54 PR agency contracts between 2003 and 2005. This covered 14 contracts worth a total of $1.2 million for the production of video news releases (VNRs) on behalf of the U.S. Census Bureau, the Food and Drug Administration, the National Institutes of Health, the Transportation Safety Administration, the National Park Service and the U.S. Mint. The main problem with these VNRs was that they were shaped as genuine news stories without proper source identification (the fault should've gone to the TV stations that ran them, but the agencies were the ones that got the heat).

But as they say in the polar world, that's just the tip of the iceberg. The GAO report only covered seven of 15 cabinet-level departments. Absent from that was the Department of Education and its Armstrong Williams subcontract to promote the Bush administration's No Child Left Behind initiative.

The Williams story deserves retelling because it details how easy it is to jettison ethics in pursuit of spin. The scandal began when *USA Today* (working with documents obtained under the Freedom of Information Act) published an article in January 2005 reporting Williams was paid $240,000 to promote the No Child Left Behind initiative in his syndicated column and TV talk show appearances and to coordinate support of the program among African-American journalists. (Williams was not considered an A-list commentator of a Rush Limbaugh or Sean Hannity level, but he was one of the relatively few prominent African-American conservative pundits, and thus his input was sought because President Bush's popularity with the African-American community was fairly low.) The contract was actually part of a larger deal ($1 million, to be exact) between the Department of Education and the public relations agency Ketchum.

When the story broke, it created serious reverberations across all lines. Williams' contract with Tribune Media Services was promptly terminated, and he became a pariah within the media industry. The White House, through its press secretary Scott McClellan, tried to dodge all inquiries into the matter. Ketchum's standing within the PR industry fell considerably, to the point that Richard Edelman, CEO of the rival agency Edelman Public Relations, wrote in his blog that Ketchum's actions resembled the "kind of pay for play public relations [that] takes us back in time to the days of the press agent who would drop off the new record album and $10 to the deejay."

Later that same month, similar PR shenanigans involving the Bush administration emerged: nationally syndicated columnists Maggie Gallagher and Michael McManus profited from the Department of Health and Human Services for supporting the White House's "healthy marriage."

Also absent from the GAO report was the Department of Defense, which got caught in late 2005 in a very bizarre scandal: it was revealed the department hired a Washington, D.C.-based PR agency called The Lincoln Group to write phony "good news" stories for placement in Iraqi newspapers. The idea behind that scheme was to shore up support for the American occupation of Iraq by having the seemingly independent Iraqi media tell the local population about the great job the U.S. troops were doing. Needless to say, no one in Iraq was fooled.

Nor was that the first time the Bush administration used the Department of Defense to try to skew public opinion in its handling of Iraq. In October 2003, a PR campaign to boost the value of the U.S. occupation of Iraq was unveiled when Lt. Col. Dominic Caraccilo, an Army battalion commander, took responsibility for a botched campaign that sent hundreds of identical letters to the local newspapers covering the hometowns of soldiers under his command. Caraccilo told the media he was eager to highlight his unit's Iraq-based activities and "share that pride with people back home" – which he accomplished by sending 500 identical form letters with different signatures. Whether Caraccilo came up with that scheme on his own was never answered, and he was promptly withdrawn from the media spotlight after the story broke.

Spin City, Part Two

Of course, spin isn't unique to Washington. The corporate world has been spinning for some time.

The tobacco industry is the emperor of corporate spin. We can trace that back to 1952, when *Reader's Digest* ran an article "Cancer by the Carton" that linked smoking and lung cancer. The following year, a report by Dr. Ernst L. Wynder confirmed that link. More press coverage on the subject suddenly began to appear and cigarette sales began to fall.

To fight back, the tobacco companies turned to PR. Leading their campaign was John Hill, the founder of Hill & Knowlton, who sought to reshape the debate via dubious science. Under Hill's planning, the Tobacco Institute Research Committee (later called The Council for Tobacco Research) was formed to refute the smoking-cancer link. This was first achieved by slicing and dicing all existing literature on the subject into a misleading 18-page booklet called "A Scientific Perspective on the Cigarette Controversy," which was sent to more than 200,000 people (including the news media, the medical profession and Congress).

In 1963, Hill & Knowlton helped create a PR and lobbying organization, the Tobacco Institute, to ensure Capitol Hill didn't legislate against the tobacco industry. It remains a formidable presence in Washington. The industry also has cultivated grassroots support via phony groups like the "National Smokers Alliance" (developed by the PR giant Burson-Marsteller with funding from Philip Morris) to ensure the "rights of smokers." To this day, the tobacco industry's PR machinations are viewed as being among the most effective.

But the tobacco industry is not unique in its history of spin. The chemical industry's PR machinery went even further in 1962 when Rachel Carson's book *Silent Spring* was published. An eloquent examination of how the indiscriminate use of pesticides was destroying the ecosystem, *Silent Spring* was credited as launching the modern environmental movement. But the chemical industry, which relied on the profits from pesticide sales, used its PR muscle to discredit the book and its author.

Time Magazine recalled the brouhaha in a 1999 article honoring Carson's accomplishments: "Carson was violently assailed by threats of lawsuits and derision, including suggestions that this meticulous scientist was a 'hysterical woman' unqualified to write such a book. A huge counterattack was organized and led by Monsanto, Velsicol, American Cyanamid – indeed, the whole chemical industry – duly supported by the Agriculture Department as well as the more cautious in the media."

Attempts were made by the chemical industry to pressure Houghton Mifflin, Carson's publisher, to halt the release of *Silent Spring*. The publisher did not bend. The rest, of course, is history.

And, of course, corporate spin continues. A recent example popped up in January 2007 when the Union of Concerned Scientists, a watchdog group, held a press conference accusing ExxonMobil of spending $16 million to finance 43 organizations that openly question global warming. The scientists charged the energy giant with attempting to manufacture doubts on the veracity of global warming. If anything, ExxonMobil was diverse in where its money went: from a $1.6 million deposit in the American Enterprise Institute, a right-wing think tank in Washington, to $30,000 for something called Africa Fighting Malaria, which uses its web site to argue against action on climate change.

"Needless to say, the practices by these PR experts resulted in the industry wearing a self-inflicted black eye," says J. Brooks Christol, corporate communications specialist at Healthways in Nashville. "The industry is facing the same issues that we've neglected to resolve throughout our history. We provide counsel to the greatest governments and corporations on how to maintain and improve their reputation and credibility, yet to the general public our industry is still seen as 'spin doctors,' a moniker far worse than any given to advertisers. While the industry often plays the role of the scapegoat for all that is wrong with the world, it is more precisely viewed as deceptive and sly. And the truth is, because of our umbilical to the news media, a few bad apples rise quickly to the public conscious that reflect upon the whole bushel. One of the current issues facing our industry is the questioning of our ethics. The forerunners of the industry knew very well that we often walked on the edge of what many consider to be ethical. Now, accepted practices have come into question by interest groups, often making us weary of how information submitted in the public interest will be perceived."

For Paul Maccabee of the Maccabee Group, the PR industry is at a major crossroads, with ethical lapses and deliberate misinformation campaigns often getting in the way of responsible operations.

"The increasingly artful use of public relations techniques like the seemingly spontaneous 'grassroots' groups are actually camouflage for partisan industry groups designed expressly to deceive the public so that corporations can achieve the highest profitability while avoiding the penalty for corporate malfeasance," he says. "The provenance of a PR campaign, as compared to advertising, is often invisible to public view. In other words, a VNR report seems like it's independently-produced news when it's actually prepared by the subject of the story; a grassroots 'smoker's rights' group may actually be a front for the tobacco industry, and that unbiased TV journalist extolling a flawed governmental program could well be in the pocket of a PR agency.

"To my mind," continues Maccabee, "the post-Sarbanes-Oxley [Act] push for corporate transparency challenges some of how PR is currently performed. The drum-beat of ethical violations by the PR industry continues, with the Center for Media and Democracy finding that 77 TV stations broadcast VNRs without disclosing the source of the material they were airing; a well-known PR agency's outlandishly fake 'Wal-Mart Across America' blog; and another PR agency's arrangement of $240,000 in payments to columnist Armstrong Williams to promote the Bush administration's Department of Education No Child Left Behind campaign, a deceptive exercise which Congressional investigators concluded amounted to covert propaganda. What's more, because PR is increasingly expensive, the power of PR all too often is available disproportionately to multi-million-dollar corporate interests while the vital messages of public interest groups, non-profits and consumer advocates are drowned out by massively-funded PR campaigns whose tools may be out-of-reach for these dissenting voices (i.e., McDonald's has more to spend on PR than anti-fast food advocates, and the tobacco industry has more PR professionals on tap than anti-smoking advocates). The result is evident in media coverage: a 2006 *U.S. News & World Report* article on the safety of nuclear power quoted six spokespeople, each and every one of them a supporter of nuclear power such as PR spokespeople from the Nuclear Energy Institute – with not a single quote from an environmental or public interest group opposed to nuclear power."

Maccabee also notes PR is not exactly a self-governing industry in regard to its bad apples. "In contrast to the medical and legal professions, which have professional disciplinary boards and ethics rules with consequences given for violations, the PR industry has virtually no professional oversight on PR practitioners who violate ethics rules," he observes. "The very fact that PR executives and PR agencies who have served the tobacco industry are still active members of the Public Relations Society of America is proof enough that the PR industry has been derelict in its responsibilities to ensure that its members do not use PR to defraud the public."

MEASURING MEASUREMENT

There is much talk within PR about measurement. Some people might say there is too much talk – entire conferences and online resources are devoted to the subject. A few trade journals devote endless amounts of editorial space to pondering the subject of measurement, writing about it with such awe and mystery that it seems on par with the Kabbalah in its complexities and mysteries. There are even a number of characters running around the industry that claim to be specialists in this subject – and I use the word "characters" without irony because these people are making a nice living telling their peers the most obvious information imaginable.

What is "measurement"? The definition, truth be told, is painfully simple. PR measurement is simply trying to keep track of the quality of the PR work and its quantifiable returns. Notice I said "quality of the PR work" rather than "quality and quantity." Quality and quantity, as any honest PR expert will confirm, are not synonymous. A PR campaign can generate hundreds of news clippings, but if they don't bring about the desired results then they simply represent an excess of valueless ink.

To be frank and cruel, measurement is PR 101. Or maybe it's PR 050, considering its focus is still heavily skewered on media relations (which, as we will see later in this book, is only part of the PR puzzle – and, as the new PR evolves, it becomes an increasingly smaller piece).

How serious is this issue? If you believe some people, it is on par with global warming. I've waded through the numerous articles, blogs and conference sessions devoted solely to

PHIL'S INSIDER PR TIP 2 A Question of Ethics

When I was running my own PR agency, a client wanted me to concoct a strategy that would be used to demean one of his competitors. The goal of that strategy would be to ruin the competitor's reputation and damage his bottom line. I refused and promptly dropped my client like the proverbial hot potato.

Other PR professionals might have taken a different approach, but that's their modus operandi. From my perspective, any project that generates the tiniest tinge of guilt or concern should be the clarion call that a major ethical mishap is in the works. The smart PR person is the one who chooses not to demean his skills or connection in pursuit of a strategy designed to create intentional suffering (whether emotional, financial or otherwise).

There is a reason why the ethical climate of PR has created problems for the industry. A good place to reverse that climate deterioration is to remember the basic lessons of right and wrong, and then act accordingly.

Okay, now it's time to get off the soapbox and get back to the chapter.

making sense of measurement, and the subject is viewed with such acute seriousness that you'd think the fate of the industry depended on the ability to measure PR activity.

To be frank and cruel, measurement is PR 101. Or maybe it's PR 050, considering its focus is still heavily skewered on media relations (which, as we will see later in this book, is only part of the PR puzzle – and, as the new PR evolves, it becomes an increasingly smaller piece). But to amuse those who need to be comforted on the subject, here are some of the main concerns relating to measurement.

◆ **KEEPING TRACK OF MEDIA COVERAGE IS TOO EASY.** There is no shortage of clipping services, monitoring services and search engines that can keep you updated on the latest coverage relating to your current PR project. None of them are infallible, but on the whole they do a fine job and usually catch most of the coverage that's out there.

◆ **YOU CAN CONFIRM THE QUALITY OF YOUR MEASURED SUCCESS BY SYNCHRONIZING IT WITH RECORDED SALES ACTIVITY, WEB TRAFFIC, STOCK ACTIVITY AND/OR CONSUMER OR B2B (BUSINESS-TO-BUSINESS) INQUIRIES THAT OCCUR THE MOMENT YOUR PR EFFORTS TAKE OFF.** This is really too easy, though many PR "experts" insist it is extremely difficult. It is difficult only if the PR person doesn't ask the sales people and webmasters to keep track of activity relating to a particular PR happening or news event. Honestly, is it difficult to piece together product sales levels, web traffic, telephone inquiries or the audience turnout for a special event after a PR-related story or promotion occurs? And if the company in question is publicly traded, how difficult is it to keep track of stock activity after corporate-related news is set loose into the information stream?

◆ **FUDGING THE TRUTH ON THE QUALITY OF COVERAGE.** This happens too frequently on the agency side of PR, when the guns-for-hire have to explain the lack of high-profile coverage. The answer is to play up insignificant coverage and pretend it is something special. Measurement gets skewered when activity reports are thick with "hits" coming from low-power TV and radio stations and publications in second- or third-tier markets. Again, quantity is being substituted for quality – and if the level of attention isn't met with a level of activity resulting from the attention, then the perception of PR's ability suffers accordingly.

From a personal perspective: I never had an issue with measurement, nor did I wind up in situations where I could not provide an accurate measurement of how the PR effort aided the corporate goals. I have problems fathoming how PR professionals are flummoxed when they are required to present a detailed measurement of their work. In the new PR environment, those who cannot measure the effectiveness of their work will be out of work – and rightfully so.

A QUESTION OF DIVERSITY

Within PR, the concept of a diverse workplace is a lot like the weather – everyone talks about it, but no one does anything about it. Okay, that's a bad joke. And diversity within PR is also a bad joke.

During 2004 and 2005, the Public Relations Society of America conducted a survey of African-American and Hispanic PR professionals to measure their perception of diversity within the industry. The survey found job satisfaction among African-American and Hispanic professionals was lower than job satisfaction among whites: only 45.8 percent of the respondents felt satisfied or very satisfied with their jobs, while 54 percent stated they experienced subtle discrimination by current or past employers and 40 percent experienced overt discrimination.

The most common problem (reported by 62 percent of those polled) came in the perception they were more qualified for positions than white counterparts, who ultimately got the plum jobs. Additionally, 60 percent felt non-white practitioners were intentionally put on slow-moving career tracks and 56 percent felt they were too frequently relegated to relatively menial tasks.

The survey also presented the following recommendations on improving diversity in PR. According to those surveyed, the primary barriers to a diverse PR environment were:

- The PR industry's lack of persuasive recruitment campaigns to attract non-white employees.

- PR recruiters being clueless in locating non-white candidates.

- Qualified candidates not knowing about PR as a profession.

"This has been a big problem for years but continues to receive little more than lip service," says Steve Cody, managing director for the New York agency Peppercom. "It's my belief that, until clients start forcing agencies to become more diverse, we won't. The bigger picture, longer-range threat is that corporations will eventually only hire those firms whose workforce reflects and understands the diverse population they themselves are trying to reach."

And that's just on the subject of racial and ethnic diversity. Gender diversity is another matter.

PR has traditionally been an accommodating industry for women. In 1960, 25 percent of the PRSA's membership were women. Forty years later, the PRSA had a 60 percent female membership.

But where are the women in PR? A January 2006 report from the Public Relations Coalition polled 73 corporate communications heads within major companies and CEOs of major PR agencies. That survey found only 38 percent of senior PR positions were held by women. Considering the high number of women working in PR, the relatively low number of women at senior levels suggests a mathematical imbalance in need of addressing.

A SENSE OF PURPOSE

In November 2005, the CMO (Chief Marketing Officer) Council released a survey that found the marketing-communications crowd (including PR executives) was not pleased with its job performance. Polling 400 executives, 10 percent of the respondents said their marketing operations were "highly influential and strategic" within the company. Less than half said their teams were "well regarded and respected" within their corporate settings.

"This study confirms marketers need to move from a tactical orientation to a more analytic and strategic approach that will enable them to realign marketing initiatives with the overall corporate mission," said Donovan Neale-May, executive director of the CMO Council, in a news release that accompanied the announcement of the survey.

In May 2006, the CMO Council released another survey. This was called "Select & Connect: Strategies for Targeted Acquisition and Retention" and it polled more than 550 marketers. The results: approximately

> *Marketers need to move from a tactical orientation to a more analytic and strategic approach that will enable them to realign marketing initiatives with the overall corporate mission.*
> —**Donovan Neale-May**

75 percent of the respondents did not have a customer advisory board or council. For the 25 percent who did, only 6 percent said the board was "very critical" for product innovation.

Furthermore, nearly 75 percent of the respondents stated they did not manage a formal online community of users or buyers, and more than 66 percent said they did not have a formal customer word-of-mouth program in place.

If there seems to be a sense of disconnect going on here, then consider the January 2006 survey of 117 PR professionals conducted by Charet & Associates. The survey found that 70.1 percent of the respondents were "extremely satisfied" in their work and 46.2 percent said it was the "best job they ever had"; six out of 10 were satisfied with their access to top management and/or key managers.

However, nearly half of those polled complained about limited advancement opportunities within their companies while only a scant 3.4 percent said they felt they'd "retire as an employee" at their current place of employment.

Dissatisfaction within the PR industry is not a brand new development. In 2002, Workinpr.com conducted a "State of the Industry Survey" of 800 public relations professionals. The results bear repeating:

◆ 85 percent of employers said they would hire a PR free-lancer versus filling a full-time in-house position. Why? Because they were cheaper to pay, more flexible in their work, and (from the employer's perspective) better for "short- term situations, employment and projects."

◆ When asked to identify the top skills and characteristics they seek in senior-level PR hires, employers ranked:

1) Project management skills – 23 percent
2) Business development skills – 18 percent
3) Personality/culture fit – 17 percent
4) Management experience – 15 percent

◆ The majority of employees (54 percent) stated that they are only "somewhat" satisfied in their current positions, while 19 percent of employees were "extremely satisfied" and 16 percent were not satisfied at all in their current positions.

◆ The majority of employees surveyed (58 percent) planned to leave their current employer within a year. When asked why, 21 percent said it was because of "a lack of challenge within their current position," while 15 percent said they would leave for a higher salary and 11 percent stated it was due to poor leadership/lack of company direction.

If PR professionals are unhappy as being a part of the larger office environment, does that mean more people will create their own agencies? No statistics exist on whether there is a trend towards PR entrepreneurship, but empirical evidence would suggest that the D.I.Y. approach is gaining popularity.

"There is always that imbalance of job dissatisfaction and the inability to take risks," observes Darren Paul, managing director of Night Agency in New York. "If people were more risk prone, everyone would start their own agency. It is a huge leap, and many people enjoy the security of a job. But more and more start-up agencies are popping up. I'd be curious to know how many more start-up agencies there were in the last three years versus the previous 10."

Adds Jay Stuck of BrandGuy Inc., who began his own agency in 2006: "The entrepreneurial spirit exists in most people but it's stifled by the need to eat and be able to afford lodging. That's why most people settle for the safe environment of a paycheck direct deposited every two weeks. And that's okay – I did it myself for 30 years. But after my 1,000th PowerPoint presentation to senior management on internal and external communications program costs, I decided to get back to my roots. No, not exactly going back to my old neighborhood in Detroit – I grew up on 8 Mile Road – but instead I opted to open my own PR agency. And you know what – it's great! I'm writing again. I'm feeling creative again. I'm screwing up again in ways I didn't think possible. And it's all terrific. Do I long for the bi-weekly paycheck? Surprisingly, no. Because I believe I'm going to make more money and be more satisfied with my work than I ever have been by being my own boss."

POINTS TO REMEMBER

Public relations is both in a constant state of change and constantly repeating itself. The tools of the trade may be more sophisticated today (and it will be amusing when future generations look back at the primitivism of RSS feeds or blogs!), but the goals and the means to those ends haven't changed that much.

The history lesson that began this chapter should be recalled the next time you are planning a PR strategy, if only to confirm the notion that success is possible by daring to take chances. Admittedly, there have been plenty of PR misfires and duds – and people can easily learn from those errors. But at the same time, the willingness and audacity to raise the proverbial bar and employ vibrant imagination to a campaign should be mission critical to any endeavor.

Imagine if Barnum decided not to bring Jenny Lind to America, or if William McKinley decided not to use the telephone for his presidential campaign outreach, or if Franklin D. Roosevelt didn't give a fireside chat. Yes, those are historic examples – but they are also contemporary examples to inspire anyone plotting a celebrity PR campaign, or considering the use of a new technology to spread a message, or to bypass the media and communicate directly with the public.

William Shakespeare once wrote: "What is past is prologue." In the case of the PR universe, Shakespeare's quote is a bit off. In PR, what is past is very much present. And while we're tossing quotes around, don't forget the pithy comment from George Santayana: "Those who forget history are doomed to repeat it."

"Don't believe your own publicity. You can't; you'll start thinking that you're better than you are."

—**Leif Garrett**

3

John Donne once wrote that "no man is an island," and that observation was more than mere topographical cleverness. As a vocation that demands constant human interaction, those working in PR can benefit from being an active part of their professional community.

The PR industry has a wealth of resources available for those seeking to share ideas (or "borrow" strategies) from their peers and to participate in the core foundations of the profession's standing within the economy as a whole. This chapter presents the numerous outlets and opportunities available for those seeking to touch base, gain knowledge and perhaps make a name for oneself within the PR spectrum.

TRADE ASSOCIATIONS

There is no shortage of national organizations devoted to advancement of PR. The majority of these organizations have conferences and publications that enable a greater sense of interconnection within the industry, and some have award competitions for those who wish to trumpet their best work.

For those who need to go out into the PR world, here are the best national organizations to get involved with – and the emphasis is on "national," because many states and cities have their own PR trade groups. Due to space limitations the local organizations cannot be listed here. Readers interested in connecting on a local level are advised to check with the following national groups to identify regional chapters.

African-American Public Relations Collective (WWW.THEAAPRC.COM)

This national network of more than 1,000 communications professionals focuses on the career advancement of African-Americans within the industry.

American Association of Political Consultants (WWW.THEAAPC.ORG)

For those interested in the public affairs side of PR, this organization gathers like-minded individuals together for a fellowship of politically tinged communications.

American Marketing Association (WWW.MARKETINGPOWER.COM)

A global organization for marketers, boasting more than 38,000 members; PR is part of its mix.

Arthur W. Page Society (WWW.AWPAGESOCIETY.COM)

This organization defines itself as bringing together "senior communications executives representing a wide spectrum of industries who are interested in helping each other and perpetuating the high professional standards set by Arthur W. Page." (Page, as you may remember from Chapter Two, was a corporate communications pioneer in the mid-20th century.)

Asian American Advertising and Public Relations Alliance (WWW.AAAPRA.ORG)

AAAPRA brings together Asian American professionals in advertising, public relations and marketing, with the mission of professional advance and solidarity for this demographic within the communications industry.

Association for Education in Journalism and Mass Communication - Public Relations Division (WWW.LAMAR.COLOSTATE.EDU/~AEJMCPR/)

Billed as the largest organization of public relations educators in the world, this group represents more than 500 academics from the United States and two dozen countries.

Association of Women in Communications (WWW.WOMCOM.ORG)

A trade organization exclusively for female mar-com professionals (sorry, guys).

Business Marketing Association (WWW.MARKETING.ORG)

Begun in 1922 as the National Industrial Advertising Association, this organization represents professionals in the business-to-business marketing and communications industries.

Canadian Public Relations Society (WWW.CPRS.CA)

The national trade association for PR professionals up north.

Center for Corporate Social Responsibility at Boston College (WWW.BCCCC.NET)

This membership-based research organization works with global corporations to help them define, plan and operationalize their corporate citizenship.

Center for Risk Communication (WWW.CENTERFORRISKCOMMUNICATION.COM)

This organization disseminates strategies and techniques to meet public and organizational communication challenges posed by public perceptions and misperceptions of risks and benefits.

CMO Council (www.cmocouncil.com)

CMO stands for Chief Marketing Officer, whose bailiwick should include PR. If the CMO acronym isn't ubiquitous in corporate America yet, give it time – this organization is working to bring marketing professionals to the C-Suite table.

CMO Institute (www.chiefmarketingofficer.com)

The organization defines its mission as being "dedicated to serving as the premier resource for researchers and practitioners interested in the role and leadership challenges facing the CMO and other marketing executives."

Corporate Communication Institute at Fairleigh Dickinson University (www.corporatecomm.org)

This organization seeks to disseminate information and theories for corporate communications practitioners.

Council of Communication Management (www.ccmconnection.com)

This nonprofit hosts a network of several hundred senior communicators, representing companies and consultancies of all sizes. Its goals are to confront strategic communications issues within today's information-clogged society.

Council of Public Relations Firms (www.prfirms.org)

This association of PR agencies seeks to raise the bar of quality through advocacy efforts, special events and publications (including international travel to explore PR initiatives in other countries) and the development of high professional standards.

Direct Marketing Association (www.the-dma.org)

Here's a global trade association of business and nonprofit organizations that uses and supports direct marketing tools and techniques.

eMail Experience Council (WWW.EMAILEXPERIENCE.ORG)

This global organization sees its mission as striving "to enhance the image of email marketing and communications."

Entertainment Publicists Professional Society
(WWW.EPPSONLINE.ORG)

This organization is the professional association for PR experts dealing in the realm of show business.

Forrester's CMO Group
(WWW.FORRESTER.COM/LEADERSHIPBOARDS/CMOGROUP/)

This subsidiary of Forrester Research is described by the company as "an executive peer network (consisting of) marketing leaders of billion-dollar-plus companies ... (who) examine key issues, evaluate new marketing tools and techniques, and marry these dynamic elements to improve decision making and accelerate marketing results."

Global Public Affairs Institute (WWW.GPAI.ORG)

This organization seeks to present an ongoing forum and information resource relating to the current and future international corporate public affairs issues and practices relating to its member organizations.

Hispanic Public Relations Association (WWW.HPRA-USA.COM)

This group advocates the career advancement of Hispanic PR professionals with educational seminars and workshops held throughout the year.

Hospitality Sales and Marketing Association International
(WWW.HSMAI.ORG)

This trade group is for communications professionals in the tourism, travel and hospitality industries.

Institute for Public Relations (WWW.INSTITUTEFORPR.COM)

For more than a half-century, the Institute for Public Relations has successfully promoted academic and professional excellence in the field through professional development forums, national competitions and special events.

International Association of Business Communicators (WWW.IABC.COM)

This globally focused organization offers products, activities and networking opportunities for people and organizations involved in PR, marketing, public affairs and employee communications.

International Public Relations Association (WWW.IPRANET.ORG)

Another globally focused organization, this group promotes the practice of international PR and seeks to bridge cultural boundaries through special conferences.

Internet Marketing Association (WWW.IMANETWORK.ORG)

This group is designed for those involved in the creation and execution of Internet marketing strategies.

Issue Management Council (WWW.ISSUEMANAGEMENT.ORG)

This association defines itself as "the professional membership organization for people whose work is managing issues and those who wish to advance the discipline."

Lagrant Foundation (WWW.LAGRANTFOUNDATION.ORG)

The mission of this nonprofit is to increase the number of non-white professionals in PR and related fields via scholarships, educational support, career advisement, mentors, internships and other resources.

League of American Communications Professionals
(WWW.LACP.COM)

An organization that, according to its web site, "encourages excellence in the practice of communications for all organizations."

Mobile Marketing Association (WWW.MMAGLOBAL.COM)

An international association with the goal of stimulating the growth of telephonic mobile marketing and its associated technologies.

National Association of Government Communicators
(WWW.NAGC.COM)

This organization defines itself as the "national not-for-profit professional network of federal, state and local government employees who disseminate information within and outside government."

National Black Public Relations Society (WWW.NBPRS.ORG)

This organization seeks to broaden career advancement via education and networking opportunities for African-Americans.

National Council for Marketing & Public Relations (WWW.NCMPR.ORG)

This is the trade association for marketing communications and public relations professionals in post-secondary education.

National Investor Relations Institute (WWW.NIRI.ORG)

This trade association focuses on corporate officers and consultants involved in investor relations practices.

National School Public Relations Association (WWW.NSPRA.ORG)

This organization is the professional society for communicators serving the nation's educational institutions and services.

Public Affairs Council (WWW.PAC.ORG)

This association focuses on communications efforts designed to influence political activity and government policies.

Public Relations Society of America (WWW.PRSA.ORG)

This group is widely regarded as the leading national trade association for the industry. Within its broad forum of services and events are two subsidiary organizations: the PRSA Counselors Academy (WWW.PRSA-COUNSELORS.ORG), which seeks to coordinate personal and professional development opportunities and mentoring between career newcomers and senior-level practitioners, and the Public Relations Student Society of America (WWW.PRSSA.ORG), which encourages college and university students at 270 campuses in a greater understanding of current theories and procedures of the profession.

Religion Communicators Council
(WWW.RELIGIONCOMMUNICATORS.ORG)

This nonprofit unites communications professionals from a diverse group of faith-based organizations.

Southern Public Relations Federation (WWW.SPRF.ORG)

This network links professionals from Alabama, North Florida, Louisiana and Mississippi; it is the only regional PR association to cover multiple states.

Web Marketing Association
(WWW.WEBMARKETINGASSOCIATION.ORG)

This group defines its mission as setting "a high standard for Internet marketing and web development."

Women Executives in Public Relations (WWW.WEPR.ORG)

This organization is designed to fuel career advancement of female public relations professionals.

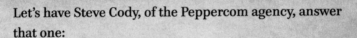

PHIL'S INSIDER PR TIP 3 <u>Association Membership</u>

Okay, that's quite a list of trade associations – but is it really worth the bother to join any of them?

Let's have Steve Cody, of the Peppercom agency, answer that one:

"I am president of the PRSA Counselors Academy. I sit on the board of the Council of PR firms, and I am a member of the Arthur W. Page Society. Each has been instrumental to my development and my firm's success but in different ways. The Counselors Academy has provided me with any number of solid, new business leads from fellow members. The Council of PR Firms has enabled me to raise the profile of my firm among the rest of the industry. And Page has enabled me to better understand what's keeping client-side practitioners up at night."

And let's second that with this comment from J. Brooks Christol of Healthways in Nashville:

"I have been a member of the YoungPRPros group on Yahoo! for about six years. This group is a real-world forum of more than 3,000 PR professionals from all experience levels that self-moderates itself as a no-spin zone. I have benefited greatly from my participation in the group, as I have seen others do the same."

Author's input: go back to the John Donne quote at the start of the chapter!

Word of Mouth Marketing Association (WWW.WOMMA.COM)

This national group is focused on (pardon the pun) spreading the word about viral marketing tactics and strategies.

Young PR Pros

(WWW.FINANCE.GROUPS.YAHOO.COM/GROUP/YOUNGPRPROS/)

A virtual association rather than a brick-and-mortar entity, this informal online gathering of early- to mid-career public relations professionals is designed to foster a sense of community and kinship for those who are either hovering below the executive level in the corporate world or who are ready to take the world by storm as young entrepreneurs with their own agencies.

PR TRADE MEDIA

The PR industry is not lacking for its own trade media. Either in print or online, the PR professional can easily read up on the various quirks, concerns and conundrums facing the industry. Some of these media outlets have their own conferences (both in the traditional sense and in an online exclusive setting).

Not surprisingly, there is a glut of online media that focus on PR issues. For the sake of quality control, only the best of the online world (both blogs and podcasts) are featured here. The determining factor for inclusion in this listing is whether they successfully provide a depth and scope of intelligent and mature consideration of industry, and whether they consistently present fresh material (many blogs and podcasts were not included here because they are erratically updated).

The best PR media to become acquainted with are the following:

Agency Wire (AW.PRPN.COM)

For anyone who can't decide which PR blogs are worth reading, this resource aggregates a selected number of the industry's most popular blog writers.

ArtsMarketing.org (WWW.ARTSMARKETING.ORG)

A comprehensive web portal that organizes practical arts-related marketing information in a format that is easily accessible to novice, intermediate and expert marketers alike.

Bad Pitch Blog (BADPITCH.BLOGSPOT.COM)

As its name suggests, this blog demonstrates the right way to throw a PR pitch by shining a cruel spotlight on those who didn't quite get it right.

Blog Herald (WWW.BLOGHERALD.COM)

Although not a PR-centric outlet, per se, this resource for news and commentary related to the blogosphere covers many PR-related aspects relating to the use of social media as a communications messaging avenue.

BtoB (WWW.BTOBONLINE.COM)

This trade weekly focuses on the business-to-business media industry, although it frequently covers issues relating to promotions and marketing for the publishing world.

Brandweek (WWW.BRANDWEEK.COM)

The weekly magazine that bills itself as "the source for branding news, promotion, marketing, and strategy."

Bulldog Reporter (WWW.BULLDOGREPORTER.COM)

This comprehensive resource offers tips for successful PR pitching, listings of new jobs and free ezines covering subjects including outstanding recent campaigns and insight from journalists on what they require from PR professionals.

BusinessMedia (WWW.BUSINESSMEDIAMAG.COM)

An online magazine covering B2B marketing and advertising.

Canuckflack (CANUCKFLACK.COM)

Colin McKay takes a look across the PR universe from a viewing point in Ottawa.

Communication World (WWW.IABC.COM/CW/)

The bi-monthly magazine of the International Association of Business Communicators.

Corporate Event Magazine
(WWW.EXHIBITORONLINE.COM/CORPEVENT/)

This quarterly magazine keeps track of issues, strategies and successful case studies in the corporate event marketing sphere.

CornerBar PR (WWW.CORNERBARPR.COM)

This collection of laid-back commentary on successful PR campaigns and concepts is authored by a group of well-regarded PR professionals.

CSRWire.com (WWW.CSRWIRE.COM)

This online news resource reports on trends and events within the realm of corporate social responsibility.

Daily Dog (WWW.BULLDOGREPORTER.COM/DAILYDOG/)

Bulldog Reporter's daily news wire provides information who's news within the PR and media spheres.

Delaney Report (NO WEB SITE)

This weekly four-page newsletter covers the marketing, advertising and media industries. It is also the rare publication without an online mirror site.

Desirable Roasted Coffee (ALLANJENKINS.TYPEPAD.COM)

While its name might suggest a celebration of the caffeine-rich wonder drink, Allan Jenkins' blog bills itself as "an oasis at the intersection of communication, society and technology."

Direct Magazine (WWW.DIRECTMAG.COM)

A monthly magazine covering business intelligence issues relating to online, email, print, search engine and other media.

DM News (WWW.DMNEWS.COM)

A weekly newspaper covering all aspects of the direct marketing industry.

earSHOT: The Edelman Podcast (EDELMAN.COM/RSS/PODCAST.XML)

The influential PR agency's self-produced podcast features insights from both inside and outside the company.

eMarketer (WWW.EMARKETER.COM)

This online resource provides ebusiness research, statistics, demographics and Internet usage data for online marketers.

eMarketing Talk Show (WWW.EMARKETINGTALKSHOW.COM)

A weekly Net radio program with a digital marketing focus.

Event Marketer (WWW.EVENTMARKETER.COM)

A bi-monthly magazine focusing on the experiential marketing sector, which increasingly relies on PR tools and strategies to promote brands, products and services.

Exhibitor Magazine (WWW.EXHIBITORONLINE.COM)

This monthly magazine covers the trade show and corporate event marketing industries.

The Flack (THEFLACK.BLOGSPOT.COM)

Peter Himler's blog seeks to "to shine a brighter light on the subtle role public relations plays in politics, culture, media, business and sports."

For Immediate Release (WWW.FORIMMEDIATERELEASE.BIZ)

A twice-weekly tech PR podcast featuring commentary by Shel Holtz and Neville Hobson.

Free Publicity (WWW.PUBLICITYINSIDER.COM)

Veteran PR rep Bill Stoller writes and edits this newsletter, which is aimed at business owners trying to raise their visibility in non-paid media.

Global Communicator (WWW.THEAAPRC.COM)

The monthly e-newsletter (delivered in PDF format) of the African-American Public Relations Collective.

Global PR Blog 2.0 (WWW.GLOBALPRBLOGWEEK.COM)

A round-up of original articles relating to communications tools (including blogs, podcasts and wikis) and how they relate to all aspects of communications and marketing.

HispanicMPR.com (WWW.HISPANICMPR.COM)

A marketing and public relations blog relating to the nation's fastest-growing demographic.

Holmes Report (WWW.HOLMESREPORT.COM)

Edited by Paul A. Holmes, this online resource defines itself as existing "to provide competitive insight and intelligence to public relations professionals."

Inside PR (WWW.INSIDEPR.CA)

Terry Fallis and David Jones host this weekly Canadian-based podcast program covering the ins and outs of PR.

International Journal of Communication
(IJOC.ORG/OJS/INDEX.PHP/IJOC)

An online academic journal, created by the University of Southern California's Annenberg Center, that "adheres to the highest standards of peer review and engages established and emerging scholars from anywhere in the world" in the discussion of communications theories and practices.

KD Paine's PR Measurement Blog (KDPAINE.BLOGS.COM)

KD Paine serves up theories and observations relating to measurement, often with a jolly nod to pop culture and headline-grabbing people and organizations.

Magazine Event Strategies (WWW.FOLIOMAG.COM/MES/)

A monthly newsletter covering experiential marketing strategies for the magazine publishing industry.

Marketing News
(WWW.MARKETINGPOWER.COM/CONTENT1049.PHP)

The bi-weekly magazine of the American Marketing Association.

MarketingProfs (WWW.MARKETINGPROFS.COM)

The "profs" are both professionals (as in the corporate kind) and professors (offering an academic insight to the subject).

Marketing Sherpa (WWW.MARKETINGSHERPA.COM)

Case studies and insightful interviews are the primary attraction for this comprehensive online resource.

Measuring Up (WWW.MEASURINGUPBLOG.COM)

Ed Moed's witty blog concentrates on the measurement of PR campaigns and strategies, with a focus on corporate communications.

Media Guerrilla (WWW.MGUERRILLA.COM/MEDIA_GUERRILLA/)

Mike Manuel authors this blog on the edgier aspects of tech PR, new media and marketing.

Micro Persuasion (WWW.MICROPERSUASION.COM)

Steve Rubel's blog highlights how "social media is transforming marketing, media and public relations."

Much Ado About Whatever

(MUCHADOABOUTWHATEVER.BLOGSPOT.COM)

Mike Bawden's blog is, according to its creator, "intended for marketers who are interested in new trends, ideas and products, but don't have the time or ambition to scan the hundreds of trade publications and blogs required to stay on top of it all."

New PR (NEWPR.CRISPYNEWS.COM)

This site allows users to submit PR-related articles and readers choose to vote on their popularity and relevance.

Online Public Relations Thoughts (ONLINE-PR.BLOGSPOT.COM)

Jim Horton authors this lively blog relating to all aspects of PR (pay no attention to the name of the blog, as it is not exclusively Net-oriented).

O'Dwyer's Public Relations News (WWW.ODWYERPR.COM)

Jack O'Dwyer, the iconoclastic journalist whose longevity (he's been at it since the late 1960s) has given him the title as the grand old man of the PR trade media, heads this mix of paper and digital media.

PartyLine (WWW.PARTYLINEPUBLISHING.COM)

This weekly newsletter offers a comprehensive roundup of new editorial opportunities and contacts at the nation's media outlets.

POP! PR Jots (POP-PR.BLOGSPOT.COM)

Jeremy Pepper's blog focuses on media relations and corporate communications with a decidedly sharp sense of humor and irony.

PR Couture (WWW.PRCOUTURE.COM)

Get ready for the catwalk with this online resource designed (no pun intended) for those seeking PR strategies to suit (okay, *that* was intended) the fashion industry.

PR Differently (PRDIFFERENTLY.TYPEPAD.COM)

Peter Shankman, CEO of The Geek Factory, a PR and marketing boutique firm in New York, authors this witty celebratory blog of the industry and its players.

PR News (WWW.PRNEWSONLINE.COM)

A weekly eight-page newsletter focusing on issues and concepts shaping the timbre of the PR industry.

PR Quest (PODCAST.PRTOPICS.COM)

This weekly podcast features interviews with provocative PR industry leaders.

PR Watch (WWW.PRWATCH.ORG)

The Center for Media and Democracy publishes this frequently harsh but always compelling quarterly online critique of PR practices (mostly relating to corporate and federal government activities). The same group also publishes a similar site called SourceWatch (WWW.SOURCEWATCH.ORG).

PR Week (WWW.PRWEEK.COM)

A weekly newspaper covering all aspects of the PR industry, including the dissection of major media markets.

Promo (WWW.PROMOMAGAZINE.COM)

A monthly magazine covering the promotional marketing industry.

Public Relations Chat (WWW.PUBLICRELATIONSCHAT.COM)

Not so much a media outlet as an open space to exchange commentary and observations; this online forum launched in late 2006.

Public Relations Strategist (WWW.PRSA.ORG)

The quarterly publication of the Public Relations Society of America.

Ragan's Media Relations Report (WWW.RAGAN.COM)

A weekly newsletter focusing on how PR professionals can get ink and air time, with insider advice from successful PR practitioners and the media people in their viewfinders.

Ragan Report (WWW.RAGAN.COM)

A weekly newsletter highlighting executive management issues affecting PR professionals.

RainToday.com (www.raintoday.com)

An online resource that defines itself as the destination "for insight, advice, and tools for service business rainmakers, marketers, and leaders."

RepChatter (www.repman.com/repchatter/)

This semi-monthly podcast starring Steve Cody and Ted Birkhahn of the New York agency Peppercom touches on issues relating to the PR world, the media and the overall business climate.

RepMan (www.repman.com)

Peppercom's Cody authors this blog on how corporations, government entities and high profile personalities either shine or wreck their public image.

Reputation Doctor (www.mikepaulblog.com/blog/)

Mike Paul's blog focuses exclusively on crisis control and reputation management, with advice on how communications experts can respond to crises affecting companies, government agencies or high profile individuals.

6 A.M. (www.edelman.com/speak_up/blog/)

Richard Edelman, one of the most influential executives in the PR agency orbit, provides a frank and often blunt critique of concerns and practices within all aspects of media and marketing.

Social Media Marketing Blog
(socialmediamarketing.blogspot.com)

Scott Monty's distinctive perspective on B2B implications of social media, which he defines as the convergence of marketing, advertising and PR on the Web.

Stars of PR (WWW.VOICEAMERICA.COM)

Cindy Rakowtiz, former head of PR for Hugh Hefner's Playboy operations, hosts this weekly talk show via the VOICEAMERICA.COM site.

Strumpette (WWW.STRUMPETTE.COM)

This site promotes itself as a "naked journal of the PR business." It is authored and edited by Amanda Chapel (and, for the sake of disclosure: the site features a weekly column by the author of this book).

Student PR Blog: Chris Clarke's Perspective on Public Relations and Online Communications (STUDENTPR.COM/BLOG/)

Overlooking the excess in the name of the blog and the fact that its author, Chris Clarke is no longer a student, one can enjoy the entertaining content designed by students in public relations and communications programs.

Target Marketing (WWW.TARGETMARKETINGMAG.COM)

A monthly magazine focusing on direct marketing and sales and lead generation strategies (including PR).

Voice of Corporate Citizenship

(WWW.BCCCC.NET/INDEX.CFM?FUSEACTION=PAGE.
VIEWPAGE&PAGEID=1490&NODEID=1&PARENTID=477)

The electronic monthly newsletter of the Center for Corporate Social Responsibility at Boston College.

ZimmCast (WWW.ZIMMCOMM.BIZ/ZIMMCAST.XML)

The official podcast of AgWired, a blog devoted to agricultural marketing and communications issues.

POINTS TO REMEMBER

PR is not an industry for loners. Tapping into the wealth of different opinions, experiences and practices can help enrich one's professional advancement (and, hey, it's also nice to make a few new friends along the way).

The Net has a surplus of resources to enjoy and more than a few to avoid (relax, because only the best of the digital environment was cited here). For PR professionals who want to contribute to the conversation, starting a blog is a great way to get noticed and make connections.

While it's not a bad idea to investigate membership in PR professional associations, it is imperative to also think of the bigger picture. Membership in other business-related organizations (chambers of commerce, community development groups, young professionals networks, etc.) is beneficial for anyone seeking to raise his or her visibility beyond the industry.

The Myth of Media Relations

4

I n the traditional concept of PR, the main focus of activities involves the placement of stories in the media. This was achieved by having the PR professional courting the media with the hope that the targeted journalists would respond by providing editorial coverage in their publications or broadcasts.

That was the traditional concept of PR. It is still being practiced but not as the exclusive manner of operations.

In the new PR environment, the public relations professional takes on a far more proactive and imaginative approach to media relations. Rather than courting the media, PR professionals are increasingly doing an end-run around the journalists through the use of high-tech tools and bold strategies. In some cases, this involves creating a new spectrum of media outlets specifically designed and controlled for PR purposes. In other cases, it involves detecting weaknesses within existing media operations and (for lack of a better word) exploiting them to the fullest.

In both cases, the relationship of PR professionals feeding news and information to journalists goes beyond being old-fashioned – it becomes truly antiquated.

THAT WAS THEN, THIS IS NOW...

In the old days, media relations was a one-way street. PR professionals would feed their information to journalists or news producers (either directly or by throwing press releases up on for-pay news wires with the hope that someone will read them and use them). In turn, the media folks would slice and dice the information as they saw fit and present it to their readers or broadcast audiences.

Some media outlets, mostly in the B2B press, were somewhat lazier and would run the PR information verbatim, often taking credit for what was being presented as news. From personal experience, I've seen my press releases rerun without a change in several high-profile trade journals, albeit with a reporter's byline attached to my writing (hey, not that I'm complaining – news coverage is news coverage).

Other media outlets, this time in broadcasting, are even lazier. Rather than send out reporters to get original video or audio recordings, they happily accept such recordings from the PR world and serve it up as their own. These recordings are known as video news releases (VNRs), audio news releases (ANRs) and b-roll.

(Some quick definitions are required here. VNRs are video segments produced by and distributed to broadcast media outlets, either by satellite feeds or by sending videos directly to the stations. ANRs are the radio equivalent of the VNRs. B-roll is seemingly miscellaneous video footage sent to broadcast news organizations, often designed to cover narrative gaps in a news story – for example, footage taken in a supermarket that could be used for a news segment on rising food prices.)

These digital tools of the trade have proven to be more than helpful for getting the PR message out – up to a point.

"Video and audio news releases are very specialized communications tools that can be used to express messages in a very real and very moving way," says Healthways' J. Brooks Christol. "But VNRs

> *Video and audio news releases are very specialized communications tools that can be used to express messages in a very real and very moving way.*
> — **J. Brooks Christol**

and ANRs are currently very volatile, scrutinized by interest groups for their potential influence [on] news stations to broadcast clearly biased advertisements under the guise of fair and balanced journalism. The VNR was created as an improvement on b-roll. The point was to help the distributing agency control the messaging by providing a package of video, sound bites and an idea of what the news segment would look like. The package could be put on tape or broadcast over satellite feeds to news organizations all over the world, allowing news editors the freedom to fill a newscast without needing to send reporters, producers and camera men on a cross-country trek.

"But journalists got lazy and news editors decided that airing the prepackaged releases in their entirety would not only spare budgets transporting news crews, but they could also fill news time without the need for additional personnel. Twenty-four-hour broadcasters such as CNN and MSNBC were prime targets for these packages because with so much time to fill they needed new, drive-through-style material. Newspapers had been successfully publishing press releases verbatim for decades, and essentially a VNR or ANR is just a multimedia press release."

All of this inevitably came crashing down. We'll let Christol tell that story:

"In 2004 a broadcast media outlet ran a VNR created by a U.S. government contractor," he continues. "At the end of the segment, the on-air personality said something along the lines of 'This is (name) reporting.' The personality was hired by the PR agency that produced the VNR and not an employee of the broadcasting outlet. The one word 'reporting' made all the difference to government watchdog groups who said the government was falsely influencing and manipulating the public through hired spokespeople acting as reporters. Of course the true responsibility lies with the broadcasting outlets that chose to use the release without editing or, at the very least, overdubbing a reporter's voice on top of the provided footage. Still, this is no excuse for our professional ethics.

"While we cannot control what is ultimately done with a press release, VNR or any other material and/or quotes provided to the media, maintaining relationships with those media coun-terparts is crucial to providing the public with responsible reporting and accurate information. We, as a profession, love to see our messages in the media, especially if they appear exactly how we want them to be expressed, but it is to our disadvantage if the method in which they are disseminated overshadows the meaning we want to get across."

Christol notes that pre-packaged offerings like VNRs continue to carry a bit of a stigma. "There is still tremendous debate on how to develop ethical standards around the use of prepack-aged materials, such as superimposed disclaimers (or 'supers') alerting the viewer to the source of the material," he says. "But to date, it has been left up to the collaboration and cooperation of news agencies and the message makers to determine the best way to use this tool. The VNR scandal of 2004-2005 was, in fact, much more complicated than the use of a single word."

He continued, "Its focus soon centered around the use of taxpayer dollars to 'create news' and if this was an appropriate use of money on the government's part. While the issue has passed to a simmer in the public consciousness, it is poised to return to the forefront of political controversy if we, as an industry, do not work to develop some stringent guidelines."

Patrick Ogle, media relations director for the Chicago-based DVD distributor Facets, is somewhat less diplomatic than Christol regarding this sales tool.

> There are a lot of complete scumbags who are PR people – look at all those fake newscast things PR firms roll out. How can you respect anyone who does that? They are snake oil salesmen of the worst kind.
>
> —Patrick Ogle

"There are a lot of complete scumbags who are PR people – look at all those fake newscast things PR firms roll out," he says. "How can you respect anyone who does that? They are snake oil salesmen of the worst kind."

Yet Christol points out VNRs are still very much in use. "I have seen what appears to be some cutbacks in the use of VNRs at the national level, but I believe that local news has become more savvy with their use of the economical option for filling air time," he says. "Many news organizations have been open to using scripts and prepared video segments, using employed reporters' voices on overdub. While news organizations attempt to be fair and balanced, the reality is that most VNRs are human interest stories, or simply don't have the need to research an opposing side, making an outlet's use of packaged materials to be well within their own ethical standards."

The local market usage of VNRs also has its drawbacks. "Sure, you may get 20 stations in remote DMAs – like a missile base in Wyoming – who may run some or all of your VNR (and the PR agency will proudly boast of 200,000 cumulative impressions)," says Jay Stuck at BrandGuy Inc. "But for the most part, you won't see your piece in major markets. I think the VNR and ANR companies need to pay more attention to the content of stories—try turning some clients down for a change. And to clients: you may think that a VNR sent to 1,000 media outlets on your new gear lubricant is newsworthy to the public at large, but, shockingly, it's not. Save your money for an important story worthy of video footage and listenership."

NET-BASED MARKETING

Few people who are old enough to remember what the PR world was like before the Internet are nostalgic for those days. The Internet, more than any tool, has freed up the ability to spread the word with greater speed and efficiency (and at a significantly lower cost than before).

The Internet has also been crucial because it gives PR professionals the ability to create their own media and to circumvent the established mainstream media in reaching their intended audiences.

Here's a case study on the simultaneous simplicity and sophistication that the Net can offer a PR campaign.

Florida's Broward County Library needed to raise awareness of its programs and services, but it lacked the budget for a full-blown PR campaign. Instead, it opted for an electronic strategy to reach current and potential library members. Maria Gebhardt, marketing manager for the library, explains what transpired when a new enewsletter was created and launched in this Q&A exchange.

Why did the library need to have an enewsletter? Didn't it already have a magazine called Bookings?

MARIA GEBHARDT: We wanted to inform and update people who may not always be physically in a branch of new services and upcoming events. We felt that the print magazine *Bookings* reached our customers, but marketing lacked with electronic media.

One of my major goals was to really focus on the Internet and new technology. Too often, libraries seem to concentrate on standard print pieces and signage. By pursuing the enewsletter, the web commercials through streaming video and the web site, Broward County Library is promoting to a much larger audience than ever before.

Did the enewsletter have an official name?

MARIA GEBHARDT: We did not give the enewsletter an official name. We wanted it to be a service that could change and transition with time. *Bookings* has a set format that customers expect. With the enewsletter, we drastically improved the format in 2006 and plan on constantly improving how we electronically communicate with customers.

What are the contents of a typical issue like?

MARIA GEBHARDT: The contents include major events, online tips, spotlights of new buildings such as the SR/BCC Library – the first Green building in Broward County, and interesting notes of important dates.

We try to promote events that appeal to a wide variety of people in the community as well as online services that can improve the experience on our web site.

What specific and exclusive marketing promotions have you used to date in the enewsletter?

MARIA GEBHARDT: We have promoted the enewsletter in our monthly magazine, *Bookings*, as well as on the web site and in press releases. We have also used signage in computer centers and bookmarks. I also try to weave signing up for the enewsletter into stories and promotional pieces.

Is the newsletter only for adults or is there a children's version as well?

MARIA GEBHARDT: This newsletter is really for adults. We are considering two additional newsletters: one for children and teens and one for our very impressive African-American Research Library and Cultural Center.

The final tally: the enewsletter was very inexpensive to create, with one person working 9.25 hours per month to create, proofread and distribute it. The monthly budget for this endeavor: $185. It has also been a major success, rising in circulation from its November 2004 premiere with 121 subscribers to an April 2006 subscription of 2,183.

WEB-BASED PR

In the past few years, an increasing number of entities (corporate, nonprofit, individuals, political campaigns) have used web sites as PR platforms for announcements of all nature. In early 2007, U.S. senators Barack Obama and Hillary Clinton eschewed the traditions of press conferences and used their respective web sites to announce their intentions to run for president.

But let's be frank: the average web site is ... well, average. And that's a major mistake, because the web site is the ultimate PR calling card. Whether someone taps into the web site on a regular basis or is coming to it for the first time, it should be the most attractive, easily navigated resource imaginable.

At this point, it should be noted that PR people would do well to be involved in the design of the web site. This may step on a few toes with their colleagues in the IT department, but it is essential that the PR person drive the design so the web site meets its maximum potential.

"The most common mistake made in web site design today is forgetting the purpose of creating it in the first place," explains Arron Brown, president of ANC Solutions

> *The most common mistake made in web site design today is forgetting the purpose of creating it in the first place.*
>
> **—Arron Brown**

in Riverside, Calif. "Customers come to your site for specific reason, perhaps to obtain office locations, read about upcoming sales or events, research your company, etc. Many times companies put so much fluff on their web site that they have no room for the meat. Not too long ago, I went to a major retail web site to get store information on locations and business hours. It took 15 minutes to find what turned out to be a link at the bottom near the 'fine print.' That was unacceptable to me."

A WORD ON SEARCH ENGINE OPTIMIZATION

Question: How can a PR person get a web site to be listed at the top of the major search engines? Answer: Search Engine Optimization.

"Search Engine Optimization is something we hear all the time, but these days it is more about Ethical Search Engine

Optimization," says Arron Brown. "You want people coming to your site because it is merited, not because you filled your site with hidden text hoping to lure people onto your site that are not even looking for something in your industry. This, when done properly is something you must stay on constantly. For every person who wants to be No. 1 there are a hundred more that have the same goal. Unless you are willing to pay web sites like Google the amount of money it takes to guarantee top billing, you are in for a battle, unless you are the only person in the world currently selling Chocolate Wuzzles."

SPREADING THE WORD VIA THE NET

Net-based marketing is a crucial element to the PR approach, especially in the entertainment field. As people rely on the Internet for information on the latest films, CDs, books and DVDs, savvy PR professionals are relying heavily on cyber-space to spread the word on their latest project.

When Albert Lai, partner and CFO at the New York-based Matson Films, was planning the 2005 theatrical release of "It's All Gone Pete Tong," he decided to anchor his PR push online. "We looked at all the Internet-based sites for our favorite films over the past five years and realized that they are practi-cally all the same design, layout and set of features," recalls Lai. "Most of these marketing campaigns use the Internet for a very defined set of informative needs: synopsis, trailer, cast, crew and theater locations. Independent films tend to try more unique approaches, but it remains difficult to convince people to spend dollars for extensive Internet marketing (beyond banner advertisements) when people more easily understand and accept the traditional media channels (television, radio and print). From a logistics point of view, television, radio and print are guaranteed channels of communication."

PHIL'S INSIDER PR TIP 4 Basic Web Site Design Principles

Admittedly, not every PR person is a web site design expert. To help point out what differentiates a good web site from a great web site, here is some advice by an expert in web design: Loren W. Lloyd, CEO of Lloyd Computer Services in Oshawa, Ontario. According to Lloyd, here's what you need to know.

- ◆ **KEEP YOUR WEB SITE ON FOCUS.** Know exactly what your customer is seeking – go the extra mile to find out their needs.

- ◆ **LET YOUR CUSTOMER STAY IN CONTROL WHILE VISITING YOUR SITE.** Don't invade the customer's privacy by forcing them to give out personal information in order to gain access to your public information.

- ◆ **MAKE SURE YOUR WEB SITE IS NOT FULL OF POP-UP WINDOWS.** This is extremely annoying to the customer.

- ◆ **MAKE SURE YOUR WEB SITE IS NOT SLOW IN LOADING.** No one has time to wait for your web page to fully open (and there are still a lot of people who use dial-up from their home computers).

- ◆ **MAKE SURE THE FONTS IN YOUR TEXT ARE EASY TO READ.** Really, who wants a web site that causes the customer to reach for a bottle of eye drops?

- ◆ **MAKE SURE YOUR PHONE NUMBER, EMAIL ADDRESS AND MAILING ADDRESS ARE ON YOUR WEB SITE.** A company without a clearly identifiable address is not one you want to give money.

Lai noted, though, that cyberspace had its own pitfalls –
especially from the consumer aspect. "You can assume that
a person in Kent, Ohio, will view the same 30-second spot
as the person in Queens, New York, though one might be
watching it on a 42-inch plasma while the other is watching
it on a 27-inch tube," he says. "With the Internet, there are
worries about operating systems, browsers, connection speeds,
monitor sizes, audio capabilities, etc., that can render an experience completely different for one viewer to the next, and
that's a major risk."

In creating a Net-based PR strategy, Lai needed to confront
the esoteric nature of his British film and how Americans
would react to it. "From day one we realized that the context
of the film, a DJ who lives and works in Ibiza, was a fairly
foreign concept to people in the U.S.," he says. "Even though
dance music grew out of the U.S. (New York, Chicago, San
Francisco), dance and rave really exploded in the U.K., Europe,
and elsewhere. We needed to educate the audience so that
they could, at least on a base level, relate to (the lead character) Frankie Wilde, since he is such an unlikable person.
Given the film covers a short period of Frankie's life, we felt it
was necessary to provide context not just for Frankie, but for
Max Haggar his agent, Jack Stoddart and the record label, his
Austrian bandmates Ladderhause, etc.

"We flew in the director and a number of the key cast members
and filmed new content over a period of four days in New
York City. This wasn't PR material; this was original content
to help tell the story of Frankie Wilde beyond the film. No one
we worked with had ever heard of doing this. We thought it
would only give the viewer a better appreciation for the film
before and after watching it in the theater. All this content was
digitized and used in the web sites that centered on the film
and characters. We closely integrated the Internet campaign

with promotional events and parties we had in New York, Los Angeles and San Francisco. We had different posters and post-cards that connected with each character. From an Internet perspective, we had people watch the film, and if they were excited, they helped us spread the good word on Internet sites."

Lai acknowledges this was not a project that could be done entirely in-house. "It's a challenge to do Net marketing by yourself," he states. "The most effective technique is to think about the overall marketing strategy and decide how Internet marketing can be an effective means to communicate the message. I'm sure there are instances where the Internet may not be appropriate. We worked with a number of key partners, including the Night Agency and RTMooreDesign, but the most critical factors were support from the producers, director and talent and integrating the Internet marketing into our other marketing activities."

"It's All Gone Pete Tong" opened in New York in April 2005 on a single screen and grossed more than $19,000 in its first weekend, which is highly impressive for a small art house film with no stars attached to it. "The Internet has been crucial to generating buzz about the film to both industry and viewers," Lai notes. "The most critical factor about the Internet campaign is that it can be modified relatively quickly, and near real-time statistics about usage can be obtained to help us understand awareness and what messages are working. Of course, the Internet as a repository for viewers' reactions is the ultimate test of the film. For better or for worse, the Internet marketing results in dialogue about the film, and as they say, there is no such thing as bad press."

ALL ABOUT BLOGS

Originally conceived as an outlet for so-called citizen journalists (not to mention anyone with an opinion and passable HTML skills), the blogosphere has evolved not only into a media market unto itself, but it's also turned into a PR avenue.

A 2005 study by the strategic communications firm Peppercom of more than 900 PR professionals found the majority of respondents (62 percent) saw the blogosphere as an appropriate venue for corporate communications, while 80 percent of the survey's respondents felt a corporate blog could help improve the dialogue between a company and its stakeholders, customers and employees.

This was in evidence during the 2006 Christmas season, when *The Washington Times* reported that 42 percent of American retailers were using blogs or RSS feeds (a feed of constantly updated information sent to blogs, podcasts or web sites) to spread the word on their holiday sales. Some blogs tried to give a human face to the retailers (Wal-Mart's corporate blog featured commentary from its employees), while others were more holiday-oriented (the Lands' End's holiday blog was authored by Santa Claus ... or a ho-ho-ho-heavy facsimile).

"It's definitely an opportunity to hear from customers who do want to communicate with you," said Sucharita Mulpuru, a senior analyst at Forrester Research Inc. in New York, in a *Washington Times* article. "And it's just another link to [the retailer's] web site to drive some more traffic."

However, not everyone in corporate America is on board. The Makovsky 2006 State of Corporate Blogging Survey (conducted by Harris Interactive on behalf of the New York agency Makovsky + Company) polled 150 senior executives from the Fortune 1000 to see if they were ready to embrace corporate blogs for communications purposes. They weren't. Just 5 percent of those polled were convinced to "a great extent" that corporate blogging had credibility as a communications medium, while only 3 percent saw it as a tool for brand-building technique and less than 1 percent thought it could generate sales or leads.

The survey's findings were confirmed by David Maister, author of *Managing the Professional Business Firm* and *Practice What You Preach*. In an interview with *Consulting Magazine*, Maister notes: "One simple truth is that high-level executives do not go to the Web. So, I am not getting managing partners. I am not getting CEOs of corporate companies – I am getting all the junior people inside those companies."

But that's just from the corporate side. Independent bloggers are enjoying their visibility and (in some cases) sense of power. It is estimated that a new blog is created every 7.4 seconds – that's a lot of blogs!

"Some of the greatest challenges the PR industry is faced with is blogging," says Latashia DeVeaux, president of the DeVeaux Agency in North Hollywood, Calif. "Despite an avalanche of freely available information, the truth is becoming harder to discern. Second, our economy in the U.S. is a factor. There are job opportunities, more so at entry and mid levels, but not at the higher levels. We're also faced with outsourcing to foreign countries. Jobs are becoming more specialized. The demand is for highly specialized knowledge in specific market segments."

Can PR professionals influence bloggers the same way they influence traditional media outlets? It depends on who you ask.

"Absolutely, though special care must be taken," says Nate Towne, president of Xanadu Communications in Madison, Wisc.

"While a marginal approach to a traditional media outlet might result in your message being ignored altogether or a minor bitch-slap by an editor, the stakes when dealing with a blogger are somewhat higher due to the chaotic medium in which they operate. It's critical to understand the blog, its audience and the blogger's style so you're approaching them with appropriate material they want – for the blogger, it's all about getting attention and being heard. If you can help them achieve these goals, it's likely you'll see some positive viral results online. If you tick them off by approaching them with a cookie-cutter traditional media pitch, it's quite possible you'll have a big, fat online PR mess on your hands that can grow exponentially due to the ease of linking between blogs and other non-traditional online outlets. Bloggers, as a whole, don't want to be treated like traditional media, nor do they wish to act like traditional media – if you can forge a meaningful connection between yourself and an influential blogger in your industry it can reap huge grassroots results."

"Not even a little bit," says Jeremy Bridgman, senior account executive with Ogilvy and Mather in New York. "Bloggers are piqued only if a story hits the center of a pinhole coverage area. Interviews aren't conducted; pitches are appropriate and audiences are niche; so many of the traditional tactics are not effective. If a blog is truly influential and important to a business, customers – and I would argue most are not – then personal communication on the blogger's time schedule is the only way to influence perceptions. But this can be a full-time job, and many PR people unfortunately have neither the time nor the inclination for this

> *While a marginal approach to a traditional media outlet might result in your message being ignored altogether or a minor bitch-slap by an editor, the stakes when dealing with a blogger are somewhat higher due to the chaotic medium in which they operate.*
> **—Nate Towne**

level of outreach. When it's absolutely necessary to include bloggers in the outreach campaign, then PR professionals need to be more creative and focused than usual."

From Darren Paul of the Night Agency: "Yes and no. Bloggers can be influenced with the right story, but generally, do not like the traditional pitching of stories and tend to despise press releases. And I love them. In many cases, they are the brain-children of creative and entrepreneurial people. Some of them have evolved to be highly credible businesses – while others are great for daily anecdotes and opinion."

"It is not about influencing bloggers – which is the issue for some PR firms, as they cannot see that - but about outreach," observes Jeremy Pepper of Weber Shandwick. "We never really do influence traditional media, but work with them. We cannot influence bloggers, but work with them on outreach, and work with them on stories, not unlike traditional media."

SOCIAL NETWORKING SITES

In the past few years, the phenomenon of social networking sites has created online communities of like-minded individuals. Resources like MySpace, Friendster, Facebook and LinkedIn are among the most popular social networking sites in operation.

While the emphasis was originally on "social," PR-related aspects have since taken root in these digital environments.

Typical of these efforts is the case of Robert Cheeke, a massage therapist in Portland, Oregon, who runs the VeganBodybuilding.com web site. Cheeke produces the annual Vegan Holiday Festival to bring together those who share his dietary-cultural practices. He also promotes this festival himself, albeit by default and not design.

"I don't have any training in PR or corporate communications," explains Cheeke. "I have always done my own PR for everything I do. I don't have a lot of money so I can't afford to have anyone else do it."

Cheeke's Net community, a rather specialized niche social networking resource, has more than 500 members – so there is a built-in audience for his messaging. He's also tapped into a much larger social networking resource to further spread his word.

"MySpace has been very good," he says. "I'd say 20 percent of the registered members on my web site found out about us from MySpace. I've also sold a good amount of DVDs, T-shirts and other merchandise to MySpace people. MySpace makes it easy to hit target audiences and large groups of people. It is also free and works well for me."

Social networking sites can also have unexpected PR value for smaller companies seeking to expand their business operations to younger consumers. For example, the pairing of mortgage banking and MySpace might seem on the far side of bizarre. But consider the number of people hooked up on MySpace – a reported 106 million as of September 2006 and a daily registration average of 230,000, and Alexa Internet has named it to the top 10 web sites in the world. While the site is not exclusively designed for the youth market, a disproportionate number of users are in their 20s.

Factor that in with the philosophy of the no-stone-unturned school of marketing, and the presence of mortgage banking on MySpace begins to make sense.

As of this writing, the major mortgage banking players are not currently on MySpace. But there are a good number of smaller, regional-specific lenders planting stakes. These lenders literally have nothing to lose by promoting themselves on MySpace, because it is a free service to join. But what have they gained for being there?

For Motor City Community Credit Union (MCCCU), headquartered in Windsor, Ontario, MySpace has provided a connection with an elusive demographic.

"We needed to start targeting a younger market," explains Melissa McCarty, business development/sales representative at MCCCU. "Among our members, the average age was around 52. We figured the best way to reach the younger demographic was to go directly to them – a lot of younger people don't know who we are and what we're about. Lots of younger people don't even know what a credit union is."

Keeping the Net spirit of interactivity alive, the MCCCU MySpace page is rich in conversation rather than monologues. "We've had great interaction with our friends," explains McCarty. (MySpace people who are linked to each other's pages are "friends.") "They've asked questions about credit scores. Credit scores were not something we thought about covering, so we posted information on that on our blog."

Another lender taking this marketing avenue is State Street Mortgage of Illinois. As with MCCCU, the company is using MySpace to introduce itself to a younger customer demographic.

"It's amazing how many young people are buying homes," says Bill Clanton, manager at State Street Mortgage. "Even 18-year-olds are buying homes."

Clanton also uses MySpace to clearly show how much State Street Mortgage has in common with its desired target market: at one point the company's MySpace page featured a music video of Shakira performing "Hips Don't Lie." For Clanton, the sultry singer's presence makes perfect sense in the middle of a page devoted to mortgage banking topics.

"We're just trying to be fun and show that we're real people," he explains. "We want to bond with people at more than one level and show that we're not just a suit."

But Clanton, who beefs up his hipster cred by volunteering that he rides a Harley-Davidson and wears a tie only for formal business meetings, nonetheless acknowledges he relied on an expert consultant for the Shakira video selection.

"I asked my 16-year-old daughter about that," he says with a laugh. "She hangs out with the 22-year-olds, and they're the ones buying the homes."

Brewery Credit Union also relied on a member of the youth brigade to set up shop on MySpace. "I have a MySpace account for myself, and I was showing it to my boss," recalls Kristin Zalewski, a 21-year-old member service representative at the Milwaukee-based credit union. "He thought it would be a good idea for us to have a MySpace account."

Zalewski is in charge of updating Brewery Credit Union's MySpace page, which will enable people to make direct inquiries for loan applications, including mortgages and home equity products.

None of the MySpace-active lenders can trace specific mortgage applications to MySpace, but all acknowledge that being a part of their target market's cyber-environment helps keep them relevant.

"All of the kids are on MySpace," says Clanton. "We want to be on any avenue that gets us their attention."

"No one asked specifically about that," says McCarty about MCCCU's MySpace audience. "But we're providing them with information to think about it – until such time they are ready to do so, then they'll think about us."

Indeed, the absence of the major mortgage banking companies from MySpace has been viewed as a blessing, particularly when it comes to leveling the marketing playing field without making a heavy financial investment.

"The big guys have the financial tools to advertise on radio and TV; they don't think of MySpace as a tool," says Zalewski. "We have 6,000 members and we don't have the funds to advertise that way. This is the advantage for using MySpace as a tool."

PUBLIC SERVICE ANNOUNCEMENTS

Here's a valuable tool that's primarily used by nonprofits to get free media placement in an environment designed for paid media: the public service announcement (PSA). As mentioned earlier in this book, the PSA took shape in the 1940s with a federal agency called the War Advertising Council, which was designed to mobilize the advertising industry's brainpower in support of the wartime effort. After the war ended, it became the Advertising Council and it functions as a privately funded nonprofit organization. The Advertising Council doesn't produce PSAs, but it distributes them on behalf of nonprofits and government agencies. The Advertising Council's PSAs turn up in the media (publications, radio, television, web sites) and outdoor locations including billboards and bus stops.

Prior to the 1980s' deregulation of the U.S. broadcasting industry, television and radio stations were supposed to live up to their "public trustee" by airing PSAs. In the post-deregulation era, that's not been the case, and the frequency of PSA broadcasting is considerably lower.

But that's not to say that PSAs don't turn up. In many cases, they can be linked to news events (for example, relief agencies saw a higher volume of PSA placement following Hurricane Katrina in 2005). And creative PR-savvy folks have been able to piggyback PSAs to popular entertainment.

Case in point: the National Marfan Foundation, a small nonprofit ($3 million budget and 20-person staff) with a niche cause (Marfan syndrome, which is a genetic connective tissue disorder that can be fatal if untreated). But in November 2005, that organization had two PSAs timed to the theatrical release of the film "Rent." Jonathan Larson, the composer who created "Rent," died from health complications linked to undiagnosed Marfan syndrome prior to his show's Broadway opening, hence the connection. The foundation was able to get a PSA included in the pre-screening slide show in theaters showing "Rent" and a video PSA with Anthony Rapp, one of the film's stars, in the Special Features section of the "Rent" DVD. The Anthony Rapp PSA was also distributed to television stations as part of the PR push for the film's release.

Not all PSAs are as flashy as that. Here's a case study on how a PSA campaign encouraged public awareness of orthopaedic well-being – or, in layman's terms, how to take care of your feet.

The organization behind this was the American Academy of Orthopaedic Surgeons (AAOS). In 2005, the AAOS launched a PSA TV campaign with a three-pronged approach: to generate partnerships with state orthopaedic societies, to create partnerships with other organizations interested in issues relating to bone health and fitness (especially in children), and to score free media placement in major markets.

"In order to have a successful PSA campaign, you first have to be in touch with what is happening in the world," explains Sandra R. Gordon, director of public education

> *In order to have a successful PSA campaign, you first have to be in touch with what is happening in the world.*
>
> **—Sandra R. Gordon**

and media relations for the AAOS. "You need to ask yourself: What topics are of concern to people? What topics are so relevant that a public service director will want to play your spot for their audience? Once all of that is in place, the key is having absolutely brilliant creative and the highest quality production values. This happens when you have a wonderful partnership with your advertising agency."

For the AAOS, the advertising agency was August, Lang and Husak Advertising in Bethesda, Md. "We have worked together for eight years," continues Gordon. "We get together each year with some of our orthopaedic surgeons and we brainstorm and come up with the very best ideas. Our other partner is Goodwill Communications, who distributes our multimedia campaign. You can have the best PSAs in the world, but if they don't get to the right people, they won't air."

Also on board were all of the nation's orthopaedic state societies, which agreed to participate by tagging the PSAs with their society identity in the markets where the PSAs aired.

"We are in contact with state orthopaedic societies in every one of the 50 states," says Gordon. "They all want their names on our TV PSAs. They are in contact with their local TV stations to help with placement. We provide them a list of every station where we distribute the spots so they can follow up. We have had many additional partnerships on our print

PHIL'S INSIDER PR TIP 5 <u>Product Placement</u>

If you're doing PR for a new product, think outside of the traditional product promotional strategies.

For Colleen Coplick, president of Type-A Public Relations in Vancouver, getting her consumer product clients coverage in the media was not a problem. But she scored a PR coup by getting the products included in the gift basket presented to celebrities attending the Academy Award ceremonies.

Here's Coplick's advice on achieving that hit: "Make sure to stick to real 'why your product is a good fit' rather than just throwing marketing speak at the organizers; they're just like media and the 'it's the BEST' won't work. Also, try and pair up with complimentary but not competing products or services to make your offer more tempting. With the Oscar basket we were in, we were part of a whole 'Vancouver Experience' package worth $15,000. We wouldn't

public service announcements that have made them more successful than ever: The Knee Society, the Association for Hip and Knee Surgery, The Orthopaedic Trauma Association, the Arthritis Foundation, the National Trainers' Association, the Milk Matters Campaign, etc."

Unlike many groups that complain about PSAs running in less-than-desired broadcast hours, Gordon reports the AAOS enjoyed a high-profile placement with its PSA. "We have been very successful in getting TV stations to air our PSAs during primetime," she says. "The reason for our success is that we produce our spots in 60 second, 30 second and 15 second times.

have gotten in as a standalone product because we weren't big enough, new enough, recognizable (brand wise) enough or fancy enough alone."

Go back and re-read Coplick's last sentence. The admission that the product was not strong enough to stand on its own is a brave one, and many PR people are too conceited to acknowledge a fact like that.

Another great place to promote products comes in the realm of corporate incentive gifts. There is an industry devoted to the sale and marketing of products for corporate incentive gifts, and they run the gamut from skincare to corporate jets. The Incentive Marketing Association and the Promotional Products Association are the trade groups for that industry, and they offer a great starting point for exploring PR efforts in that realm.

In addition, we have topics of local importance," Gordon adds. We have the names of state societies on the spots and we have really fun and great creative."

The PSA campaign was distributed to 1,100 broadcast stations and 500 cable stations in March 2005. "Through our distribution reports, we know that viewer-

> There is an industry devoted to the sale and marketing of products for corporate incentive gifts, and they run the gamut from skincare to corporate jets.

ship reached over three million people," says Gordon. "In addition to airing on TV, our spots are used by our members as they speak on orthopaedic conditions in their communities. They are used at meetings, they have been requested by the Surgeon General, and they have been featured at AMA meetings."

And what would've happened if the AAOS was forced to offer the PSA as a paid advertisement? The same coverage that the free media PSA received would've cost $5 million as paid advertising.

MAKE YOUR OWN MOVIES

It's one thing to gain PR points via product placement in motion pictures or TV shows. But it's quite another feat to create a movie or television show.

This is not a very common strategy, but thanks to the development of low-cost digital video equipment and the surplus of academic outlets teaching video production, PR professionals with a flair for the theatrical are able to pick up a camera and start shooting their own productions.

There is a noble history to this. Consider the 1948 feature "Louisiana Story." Most people know this is the last movie directed by Robert Flaherty, the father of documentary film-making. It is also common knowledge that "Louisiana Story" was nominated for the Academy Award for Best Original Story, was added to the Library of Congress' National Film Registry, and won the Pulitzer Prize for Music (Virgil Thomson's composition is the only film score to receive that honor).

What most people don't know, however, was that "Louisiana Story" was produced by Standard Oil. Yes, that's a company that rarely enjoyed positive PR. But with "Louisiana Story," Standard Oil commissioned a feature film that played up the pro-development aspects of oil exploration in the Louisiana Bayou.

Johnson Wax took this challenge one better with its 1964 documentary "To Be Alive!" Designed to be a celebration of the world's many cultures and the common bonds shared among peoples in all corners of the globe, "To Be Alive!" premiered at the Johnson Wax Pavilion at the New York's World Fair (it was presented on three 18-foot screens) and won a special award from the New York Film Critics Circle, the first time a non-theatrical presentation was so honored by that celebrated organization. The next year, the film played in Hollywood and it won the Oscar for Best Documentary Short Subject.

"To Be Alive!" is still playing – at SC Johnson headquarters in Racine, Wisc. The SC Johnson Golden Rondelle Theater presents the film in its original three-screen version. It reportedly still brings in visitors (no mean feat, considering the lack of tourist attractions in Racine!).

Today, lower-cost video camera equipment is enabling PR professionals to make their own films. One of the most notable examples is Novo Nordisk's documentary "Peaks and Poles: The Will Cross Story." The film focuses on the Pittsburgh mountaineer who became the first person with diabetes to climb the highest mountain on each of the seven continents and trek to the North and South Poles.

Novo Nordisk, a healthcare company that sponsored Cross, did not release the film theatrically. Instead, it used it for promotional and marketing purposes (it is available in DVD format as a 20-minute and 47-minute production). Copies of the DVD have been distributed to diabetes organizations, healthcare professionals, individuals living with diabetes and members of the company's international sales force.

Equally impressive is the four-part serial "Phished" created by the Night Agency in New York for a webcast on Symantec's Safetytown microsite. "Phished" follows the misadventures of an average Joe who discovers that his financial data has been stolen via the Net (or, in cybertalk, he's been phished). Rather than sitting around waiting for outsiders to help solve his problems, this crime victim turns crime fighter in trying to hunt down and bring to justice the miscreants who hooked him into giving up his information.

Although it is sponsored by Symantec, the anti-virus software company, "Phished" is not a commercial for the company or its product line. If anything, it is a stylish and entertaining produc-

> *That's where the power and viability of D.I.Y. film and video production works: when the production transcends the inevitable PR hunger to sell-sell-sell.*

tion that approaches the serious subject of identity theft with uncommon originality. Scott Cohn, a creative director at the Night Agency, wrote and directed "Phished" (the agency also built the Safetytown web site and coordinated an online PR campaign, thus scoring a triple play with this project).

And that's where the power and viability of D.I.Y. film and video production works: when the production transcends the inevitable PR hunger to sell-sell-sell.

In the fall of 2006, the Federal Home Loan Mortgage Corporation (better known as Freddie Mac) wanted to increase the level of homeownership among Hispanics. So Freddie Mac's creative team created a Spanish language TV *novela* exploring issues of homeownership. Promising a production where "hot storylines meet meaningful messages" (that's Freddie Mac's language, not mine), the 13-episode "Nuestro Barrio" follows the married nightclub owners Manuel and Marisol in their pursuit of the American dream house. Several independently-owned TV stations in markets with large Hispanic communities broadcast "Nuestro Barrio" as a mini-series.

The ability of Freddie Mac to get this program on the air as a regular series and *not* as an infomercial is commendable. It is still currently being broadcast via local stations, and it is also being made available to mortgage lenders on DVD as a promotional product.

Plus, the notion of marketing something as serious as homeownership within the oversexed, campy melodrama of a *novela* is fun – and how often do the words "mortgage" and "fun" wind up in the same sentence?

The D.I.Y. nature of online video is also being tapped into. Another financial services giant, ING Direct, tapped into this realm in the fall of 2006. The company launched the web site WWW.MOVEOUTMOVEUP.COM with a series of comic video clips showing sitcom-worthy hassles involved in renting while playing up the nirvana of homeownership – via the company's subsidiary Orange Mortgage.

From a PR standpoint, ING Direct's use of low comedy is refreshing – particularly the episode "Tea with Grandma," where a grandmother's visit is disrupted by the excessively passionate acrobatics of the neighbors on the other side of the thin apartment walls. The company also discovered the joys of viral video distribution, as its clips have turned up on YouTube, Yahoo! Video and other online venues.

Of course, not every in-house production is going to win an Oscar or wind up on the National Film Registry. But the truly creative PR person cannot rely on old-fashioned press releases to get the word out and connect with audiences. At a time when it is too easy to make films and videos, it should be incumbent upon all PR professionals to channel their inner Orson Welles and grab a camera.

POINTS TO REMEMBER

To be honest, journalists are not offended when PR people create their own media. They only pay attention when these efforts are morally and intellectually dishonest. Presenting a VNR to promote, say, a turtle race won't raise an eyebrow. But presenting a VNR designed to advocate a controversial political agenda in the guise of a benign puff piece raises a red flag of the deepest crimson hue.

PR professionals who wish to confirm their invaluable status would be well advised to explore the craft of D.I.Y. media production, with a strong emphasis on web design and video production. Having the ability to design and maintain web sites effectively cancels the need for an outside web designer, while being able to create original video material offers new opportunities for the promotion of products and personalities. And, hey, it could lead to the proverbial "bigger and better" – after all, if Johnson Wax can get an Oscar, why can't you?

Oh, one last word on blogs: realize that a blog that enables readers to respond can open the floodgates to potential slamming and spamming by online mischief makers. If you are going to create a blog on behalf of a corporation or organization, think twice about including the function to allow reader commentary. If readers will be allowed to post comments, then monitor the blog on a daily basis to ensure nothing rude or libelous is printed.

> *"Good communication is as stimulating as black coffee, and just as hard to sleep after."*
>
> **—Anne Morrow Lindbergh**

5

This chapter focuses on what has been called event marketing and experiential promotions. In the old days, it was known as simple direct outreach or person-to-person communications. But increasingly, it has become a major factor in shaping PR strategies.

Event marketing is important because it provides a direct channel between the company/organization/brand and its target audience. The media, which traditionally serves as the filter or middleman in this relationship, is excluded.

The events can be among the most important happenings of the year (the Super Bowl, Academy Awards, etc.), or they can be extraordinary for their sheer modesty – such as a Mississippi cookout.

"We go to a lot of community-based events," says Scot Slay, marketing and communications director for Hope Community Credit Union in Jackson, Miss. "Some of these events are really small, like 100 people. But those folks are real important to us."

Why should a PR professional consider an experiential campaign? "Why wouldn't they?" asks Rod Meade Sperry, media director for Wisdom Publications, Somerville, Mass. "It's all about familiarity. The more people interact with a brand or product, the more they 'know' it—it can become like a comfort food or a trusted authority."

Wisdom Publications offers books with Buddhist themes, which is admittedly a niche category in the United States. For Meade Sperry, experiential promotions help to get the Wisdom titles to stand out.

> *The more people interact with a brand or product, the more they 'know' it—it can become like a comfort food or a trusted authority.*
> —**Rod Meade Sperry**

"In our case, perhaps above all, we have to deal with the fact that most people do in fact judge a book by its cover," he says. "So we put a particularly strong emphasis on packaging and advertising, in a way that I don't think other Buddhist book publishers do. We'll always have a traditional approach for some of our core audience titles, but more and more often, we'll take a risk and do something that other Buddhist publishers wouldn't think of. This is not only part of our publishing strategy, in terms of acquisitions – it's part of our marketing and packaging strategies.

"A good example of this is found in the story of my work for our book *Hardcore Zen: Punk Rock, Monster Movies, and the Truth About Reality*. It's my contention that, if presented correctly, Buddhist books can appeal and hold truck with readerships that are well outside the typical Eastern Religion reader – people who are not particularly going to be turned on by the old, clichéd images of lotus flowers or water droplets and ripples. *Hardcore Zen* is a case in point. It was a Buddhist book by a punk-rock-musician-turned-legitimate-Zen-master. The book is gritty, even a little nasty at points, and so we covered it thusly. The "cover star" is in fact a toilet – the toilet of a grafitti'd, heavily flyered bathroom in what appears to be a gritty, nasty punk rock club. No one had ever done that before; the idea of a toilet on a Buddhist book seemed incomprehensible to some. Even our distributor at the time told us that it would never fly; people would be revolted.

"Instead, the cover became celebrated for being so different. It stopped people dead. And when they picked up the book and turned it over, it said: This is a book about Zen for people who don't give a rat's ass about Zen. No one, no 'thing,' had ever communicated about Buddhism, of all things, in these terms before. The effect was that they interacted with the book, were charmed by it, bought it, read it and talked and blogged about it. In book marketing, there may be no experiential goal greater than to get someone to pick your book up off the table and then flip it over and read the back. At that moment, they're only one step from owning it. It's key."

And it worked. "Instead of selling very few copies of *Hardcore Zen*, we've sold some 20,000 in the past three years," he adds.

Experiential promotions truly represent a major thrust in the PR battle plan. "It's an opportunity for them to pull closer to their consumer," explains Darren Paul of the Night Agency, which special-izes in guerrilla marketing. "People's view towards tradi-tional advertising is worse and worse each day, on top of the challenges of reaching people through mass media. That said, it is important for a brand to engage with their consumer. If a brand can then have exponential word of mouth, media and buzz – that's an added-value."

> *People's view towards traditional advertising is worse and worse each day, on top of the challenges of reaching people through mass media. That said, it is important for a brand to engage with their consumer.*
>
> —**Darren Paul**

So what are some the key points to a successful experiential marketing campaign? "It needs to leave a positive, lasting impression," continues Paul. "It needs to be relevant, and on strategy. It should appeal to the media – as one of the common goals of an experiential marketing campaign is to get media exposure." Experiential promotions cover a broad territory. Let's examine the most important sectors within this practice.

PRODUCT INTRODUCTION/PROMOTION

Is there a better way to introduce a product to its intended audience than through experiential promotions? By literally putting the product before those who need to know about it, the PR professional is able to allow the target audience to build its own impressions of the newly introduced item.

Consider the following case study on how the Coca-Cola Company launched its Full Throttle energy drink product line in 2005. Full Throttle was described by the company as "16 ounces of citrus-flavored fury in a can," and its target market was primarily blue collar men between 20 and 30. Coca-Cola determined the product needed to be branded with a macho yet good-humored image – a man's drink, but without masculine pretensions.

Coca-Cola tapped the agency Fast Horse Inc. of Minneapolis to handle the product launch. The agency's initial research for the potential target audiences was handled in one-on-one intercepts at vocational schools, construction sites and sporting venues (as opposed to other venues that may have been interested in the product).

"With limited time and budget for the research phase of the planning process, we needed to identify the most efficient way to gather insights from target consumers – young adult, blue-collar males," recalls Scott Broberg, vice president at Fast Horse Inc. "As an alternative to formal focus groups, conducting one-on-one intercepts at locations with a large cross section of blue-collar males – such as vocational schools, construction sites and sporting venues – became an effective way to secure qualitative research and validate our creative concepts."

The agency decided to use the 2005 NASCAR season to launch Full Throttle. In a way, that was somewhat daring since NASCAR has a lot of promotional activities and advertising connected to it. Yet Broberg felt this was the right venue to pursue – and to stand out from the other vehicles at the race-track, Fast Horse created custom-built motorized armchairs that would be raced by some of NASCAR's popular drivers.

"Even in the marketing-heavy world of NASCAR, the image of two celebrities racing each other in motorized armchairs created a visual compelling enough to break through the clutter," says Broberg. "In addition, we specifically held the event on the Friday before the Daytona 500, since there was little on-track activity that day after qualifying races took place for much of the week. With the lack of on-track activity to fill the NASCAR news hole heading into the weekend, our lighthearted story appealed to sports media around the country that were previewing NASCAR's first – and biggest – race of the year."

Getting NASCAR drivers to step out of their automobiles and into the motorized armchairs was not difficult. "Michael Waltrip and Greg Biffle were excited to drive the world's fastest armchairs," recalls Broberg. "Most NASCAR drivers will race anything at anytime, and in the case of the Full Throttle Armchair Challenge, Waltrip and Biffle had plenty of assurance the 'vehicles' were safe. The motorized armchairs were inspected and approved by a qualified risk management expert upon completion of the fabrication process. In addition, the builder was on-site to give the drivers a tutorial, and they were able to get familiar with the vehicles by taking a test drive prior to the event."

The motorized armchair race and post-race interviews with Waltrip and Biffle received coverage on ESPN, Comcast Sports South and the Speed Channel. Broberg also created a b-roll package featuring the event highlights for satellite distribution to TV stations across the nation. Needless to say, the b-roll made mention of the Full Throttle brand as part of the video coverage being provided.

"With a satellite truck on-site at the event, we were able to quickly edit a b-roll package and transmit the best footage and sound bites via satellite to TV stations around the country that afternoon," continues Broberg. "The majority of the campaign's broadcast coverage – more than 400 stories – was generated by the b-roll package, including segments on national outlets, such as The Weather Channel, FOX News and WGN SuperStation, as well as local affiliates in 20 of the top 25 markets, including New York, Los Angeles, Chicago, Philadelphia and Atlanta."

So how did it help Full Throttle? According to Broberg, the product achieved a 7.8 percent share of the energy drink market within four months of the NASCAR event. During that period, it also became available in more than three-quarters of all American convenience store locations. The latter statistic helped Full Throttle win the Retailer Choice Best New Product of 2005 from the convenience store trade publication *CSP Magazine*.

And what became of the motorized armchairs? "They are currently in storage," says Broberg. "We're hoping they will see the road again someday as part of a special event or grassroots campaign for the Full Throttle brand."

So what did we learn from this PR endeavor?

♦ Having direct contact with your target audience is
crucial in determining the PR and marketing strategy for
a new product launch.

♦ Creating a promotional activity that can stand out, even
in the midst of an event-heavy happening like NASCAR,
will help call attention to your endeavors.

♦ Using a sense of humor doesn't hurt, especially if it is a
gentle good-humored bit of fun.

♦ Including the product name in the promotional event is
crucial, as the media will incorporate that in its coverage
of the event.

♦ Creating your own media coverage (in this case, b-roll
footage) is a great idea because it can help you reach
media outlets that were unable to be part of the event as
it occurred.

GUERILLA MARKETING

Experiential promotional events don't need to be formally
structured. Spontaneous eruptions of PR imagination, also
known as guerrilla marketing, can engage the public in a
joyously surprising manner.

Why would a PR professional wish to include guerilla
marketing as part of her communications campaign? "I'd
suppose that many PR professionals would rather not have
to," says Rod Meade Sperry. "Guerilla marketing, to many,
connotes a shoestring budget or a desperate measure. It's also
not yet scientific: your success depends on your savvy, yes,

but you also need the right conditions. But doing something unusual or disruptive to expectations will usually make you stand out, and if you do it right, in a good way."

What are some of the key points to a successful guerilla marketing campaign? "I don't know that there is any one set of key points that could be applied," continues Meade Sperry. "Guerilla marketing, to me, indicates a more spontaneous and intuitive approach. You've put yourself in the mind of your audience and are hit with a flash 'You know what would really stop me in my tracks?' You identify a bold or odd move, and then you implement it."

While some people may mistake guerilla marketing as a spontaneous, spur-of-the-moment endeavor, it requires a great deal of planning in order for it to appear subtle and seamless.

"You need to achieve integration of the visual elements of the PR campaign with the visual elements of the experiential campaign," says Paul Maccabee at the Maccabee Group. "Our 'Human Art Gallery' PR campaign to promote OfficeMax's Ink Refill program integrated the 'tattoo' themed visuals of the pre-existing ad campaign with tattoo-themed visuals of the experiential promotional campaign snaring TV coverage on all five Chicago TV stations and on CNN-TV worldwide."

Maccabee's campaign was certainly eye-catching: having tattoo artists create temporary recreations of paintings from the Art Institute of Chicago on the bare backs of male and female models. All of this was done outdoors in downtown Chicago. For pure audacity, not to mention for the pure artistry, this campaign was a winner.

While once considered the exclusive bailiwick of smaller companies and agencies, guerilla marketing is now part of the

PR push of major corporations. For Maccabee, that may not be such a great development.

"I am disturbed about the ethical lapses of some guerilla marketing campaigns, where the corporate sponsor of the marketing campaign is camouflaged and hidden from the consumer," he says. "For example: when a pretty woman asks you to take her photo and hands you the digital camera from her employer, but no one tells you that you're being 'sold' by that digital camera company."

A word of caution: sometimes guerrilla marketing campaigns can backfire very badly. Case in point: on January 31, 2007, the city of Boston was thrown into a panic when police found small battery-powered light screens surreptitiously set up on bridges and overpasses around the city. They were thought to be terrorist bombs but turned out to be magnetic signs designed to promote a program on Cartoon Network, a division of Turner Broadcasting System.

The result was a mess. Roads and subway lines were shut down while the police investigated the devices (which were actually in place for two weeks before the police even noticed them). The two young men hired by an agency to install the signs were arrested (the Boston Police Department's PR officials made sure the men were displayed in a well-designed perp walk).

Phil Kent, chairman and chief executive of Turner Broadcasting System, summed up the result of the panic succinctly: "This is not the kind of publicity we would ever seek." The network later paid the city $2 million to settle the costs of the police investigations and activity, and Jim Samples, the head of the Cartoon Network, resigned following the brouhaha.

Thus, it is a great idea to always check with local law enforcement entities and municipal agencies before conducting guerrilla campaigns in public places that involve the installation of objects on public property.

GRASSROOTS PR

Another experiential PR strategy involves grassroots activism, in which the general population finds itself swept up and involved in the running of an effect-oriented campaign. For the most part, grassroots PR is used to spark spontaneous political movements via letter writing, protest rallies and (for those truly committed to the cause) civil disobedience. Grassroots PR also can be used to generate effects on commerce, most often through boycott and censure of products, services or presentations that people consider to be harmful or distasteful.

"Connecting with disparate audiences and demonstrating through messaging that you share similar goals are vital in the coalition building effort, which to me is the whole point of grassroots PR," says Xanadu Communications' Nate Towne. "When established and respected organizations, groups and individuals communicate your message on your behalf, you add their supporters to your ranks and exponentially increase your ability to change public perception. In addition, communications from private citizens and grassroots organizations are perceived as more influential than those from corporations who have a fiscally-vested interest, which is why grassroots PR initiatives are a valuable addition to any PR campaign."

More often than not, grassroots PR reaps a considerable harvest. But the PR professional needs to keep on top of the endeavor throughout the entire campaign.

"Grassroots PR can bring about huge results if properly researched, planned, implemented and managed," continues Towne. "Political campaigns exhibit excellent examples of successful grassroots PR efforts in action as they bring together diverse groups of lobbyists (mothers, unions, students, etc.), who share similar goals yet normally operate independently of each other. Through use of these different social factions, politicians are able to reach voters they might never have reached using messages that resonate most with each group's audience."

But at the same time, grassroots PR runs the risk of being corrupted. "The general population looks at PR negatively because all too often, public relations campaigns utilize deceptive techniques, such as grassroots groups that are actually industry-sponsored shills designed to mislead the public, to camouflage a corporation's actual behavior in the marketplace," says Paul Maccabee. "A particularly horrific example of the damage that a PR campaign can contribute to was when the A.H. Robins company used PR (aimed at magazines from *Family Circle* to *Mademoiselle*) along with advertising to convince the public that their Dalkon Shield IUD contraceptive device was safe and effective, when in fact A.H. Robins knew internally that their IUD was actually lethal and deeply flawed. The book *Nightmare: Women and the Dalkon Shield* by Susan Perry and Jim Dawson called it "a veritable case study of corporate irresponsibility" in which PR played a key role. Similarly, notorious polluters in the chemical and power industries use PR to tout their environmental records, as they continue to treat the environment with disdain; and other companies envelop themselves in breast cancer-related PR campaigns while producing the very carcinogens known to contribute to cancer. The Bush administration's cynical use of PR as a propaganda tool (specifically in relation to the Iraq War debacle, but also involving the Department of Education) has permanently associated PR with mendacity and corruption. And Wal-Mart's fake "grassroots" Working Families for Wal-Mart group and its WALMARTINGACROSSAMERICA.COM project, produced with help from Edelman, was a disaster

for Wal-Mart and a black eye for the PR industry – especially
because of the outlandish fake blogs (flogs) created by and
for Wal-Mart."

TRADE SHOW PR

In the course of many PR professionals' careers, a trade show will
pop up. More often than not, there will be a glut of trade shows.

Trade shows often represent the best of all worlds in regard to
event marketing because they cater exclusively to the core audiences you are trying to reach. Whether creating special events
at a trade show booth, or working the exhibit floor to button-
hole current and prospective clients, or sponsoring a special
gathering at the show (a party or a seminar), trade shows allow
the PR professional to have direct contact with the people who
should matter most.

Furthermore, trade shows (particularly of the B2B variety)
attract journalists from specific media outlets who should be
covering the products/services/companies you are promoting.

For Suzanne O'Leary Lopez, public relations manager at
Thornburg Mortgage Home Loans in Santa Fe, N.M., a trade
show should be worked to guarantee only the best media
coverage. "The quantity of trade interviews is only relative
to the top-tier trade publications you are targeting," she says.
"If 12 of your top-tier trade journalists are going to be there,
you definitely want to meet with all of them if you can. I don't
necessarily look at the quantity of the meetings but more of the
quality of the meetings."

But is a trade conference a good place to make a major
announcement, or is there the risk of getting lost in the shuffle
and crowds? "I believe it is a good place to make a major

announcement—the press are looking for major announcements while they are there and you have all of them together at once—I've found it to be quite effective if used strategically and timed well," says Lopez.

MOBILE MARKETING

During the past few years, one of the most popular forms of experiential promotions has been mobile marketing. By this, I am not talking about the cell phone variety of mobile marketing. Rather, I am talking about the use of special vehicles (usually of the 18-wheeler variety) that crisscross the country for PR value.

Mobile marketing is not a new concept, per se – the oldest known mobile marketing promotion involved the Oscar Meyer Wienermobile, a hot dog-shaped car first introduced in 1936. Variations on the Wienermobile have been presented over the years; and it is still on the road. The Kissmobile, a large truck featuring three humongous Hershey's Kisses, is perhaps the second-best known mobile marketing vehicle. Both the Wienermobile and Kissmobile turn up at scores of special events annually where their respective product lines are being promoted. These can include urban centers, suburban malls and even college campuses.

What are the core ingredients for a successful mobile marketing campaign? "The first ingredient is a good, solid plan," says Larry Borden, CEO of The Borden Agency, a Philadelphia company specializing in mobile marketing. "My good friend Confucius once said: 'Failing to plan is planning to fail.' You must identify what it is you want to accomplish,

> *My good friend Confucius once said: 'Failing to plan is planning to fail.'*
>
> **—Larry Borden**

PHIL'S INSIDER PR TIP 6   Trade Show PR

**What's the best way to generate media coverage
at a trade show?**

For that inquiry, I'll turn over the spotlight to Karen Friedman,
president of Karen Friedman Enterprises, Inc., a media and
communications training firm in Philadelphia. She says there
are key tenets to trade show PR that you need to recall.

"For starters, don't be fooled by thinking attracting coverage
and receiving coverage is equal. Attracting coverage at many
trade shows is actually the easy part, especially if the venue,
like the Philadelphia Flower Show, is a hometown favorite that
appeals to thousands of people. But just because reporters are
floating about, doesn't mean they'll float your way.

"Organizers plan in advance and so should you. If you have a
cool gadget, interactive media display, or plan to announce
a new product, let organizers know in advance. When a
reporter pops in and is looking for something visual or innovative, they might point the person in your direction.

"Reformatted brochures or slick annual reports do not tell
your story in a reporter-friendly format. However, your press
kit does not need to arrive with brimming balloons and
overflowing beach balls that get batted around the newsroom
and will not land you coverage. Your kit should tell your story,
provide key information and include your booth number,
media contacts and phone numbers.

"Not every trade show is a media magnet. For example, new
fillings on display at the dental convention might interest an

industry publication, but not generate much interest among mainstream media. Yet, if the latest in dental needles was completely pain free or a new brand of toothpaste really could wipe out cavities forever, your pitch will likely score more attention.

"Reporters need visuals. Put photographs, displays or posters up at your booth so they can see what you're talking about. If you're handing out photos, make sure they are high resolution and available in various formats and can be accessed on your company web site for reprint. Include short captions and photographer credits. If a reporter is attracted to your booth, visuals increase attention and provide a backdrop for interviews.

"Too often, however, public relations efforts focus very heavily on capturing media attention and fail to spend critical time understanding how to benefit from their 15 minutes of fame. As a reporter, I've walked away from many a trade show staffer who talked about his company and could not simply explain how his product would benefit or improve the lives of my viewers.

"If your staffers aren't media trained, keep them away from the trade show. They need to know what reporters want, dos and don'ts of interviewing and how to develop a short attention grabbing description that they can share with almost any audience. Don't refer the reporter to a PR person back at the office. If they walk away, chances are, they're gone for good.

(continued next page)

"Don't assume the reporter will call you to follow up. Give them a couple of days and then call to find out if they need additional information, pictures or interviews. Reporters hate to admit this, but the easier you make their job, the happier they are.

"Finally, ask the right questions. Take a moment to find out who you're talking to, what they cover and what would interest their readers or listeners. Then, try to become one of those readers and visualize what you would want to read about if you were them. When you learn to speak from an audience's perspective, you will build credibility and position yourself as someone who gets it. By doing that, you are positioning yourself as a resource, building relationships and opening opportunities for the reporter to call you in the future. That's what leveraging is all about."

how much you are willing to spend and how many people you want to impact and once you impact them, what you want them to do. Once established it's time to put the plan together. Although it sounds simple, mobile marketing is quite complex. For this reason, we recommend hiring a mobile marketing consultant or an agency to objectively review your plan and offer several solutions that will help you achieve your plan.

"A good agency will listen to you, offer several solutions, budgets, vehicle designs and program components. They will also be able to show you how their ideas will tie back into your goals and objectives. Sometimes the simplest programs will garner the best results. Don't focus too much on what other companies have done, rather focus most of your time on your unique challenges, consumer and objectives. And most importantly choose your consultant or agency wisely.

It has truly become a buyer beware market in our industry. Everyone from independents to advertising agencies is offering mobile marketing services. For the most part they call a mobile marketing expert to help them pitch new business and operate programs on their behalf. Most of the time, you don't even know they exist until there is a problem. Mobile marketing has many layers and you need a real expert on your side. Let your ad agency and trade show vendor in on the idea but ultimately only a true expert can help you avoid the common pitfalls before they happen and help lead you to solid measurable results smoother and more cost effectively then anyone else."

Mobile marketing requires a considerable number of tools, not the least being the vehicle itself. Factor in the costs associated with transportation (including fuel, insurance, personnel), and it might seem that mobile marketing is too expensive. Or is it?

"It depends on how creative you can be," continues Borden. "I've seen local printing companies retrofit small trailers so they can take their print shops to their customers; dentist's outfit UPS style vans; boutiques take their wares to the state fair; and on and on. Yes it can be costly, but so can anything else. If transportation costs are a factor, start out in one area first to see if you get the kind of return you are looking for. If it works, slowly extend the geography. If you have scattered sales regions, put the vehicle in one sales region at a time and have your sales people drive it. Bottom line: be creative. Purchase a used vehicle, lease a vehicle, have your art department design the graphics wrap, hire an intern to drive the vehicle, let your secretary manage the schedule and so on, and so on."

So what can mobile marketing offer that other traditional PR approaches cannot? "I would not look at mobile marketing as what can 'it' offer that traditional 'PR' cannot," diplomatically comments Borden. "Rather, I would look at it as 'How can mobile marketing help boost my PR initiatives?' Mobile marketing is the sacred pill that if done properly can 'boost' results. For example, Avon does an enormous amount of PR and they get good results from it. Their products are consistently in magazines and they occasionally receive television hits. The Avon Let's Talk Beauty Tour (a mobile marketing tour coordinated by The Borden Agency) is receiving 3- to 7-minute in-studio segments in major markets to discuss nothing but Avon. The tour and its components are more unique therefore more compelling then a static press release. It's an actual event. It's perceived by the media to be of importance due to the grandeur of the program, the uniqueness of the program and the offerings of the program. In conclusion, a mobile marketing campaign can enhance a PR campaign, break through the clutter of press releases and show perceived value to an editor or producer looking to fill space and time."

Mobile marketing is not strictly for consumer goods. The B2B crowd can also get in on the fun, too.

"Business-to-business marketers can benefit tremendously with mobile marketing," continues Borden. "Not only can it double as a tradeshow exhibit, PR machine, buzz builder and hospitality suite; it can also become a sales generator. For example, our client General Electric built a mobile marketing program to support their sales team across the country. Instead of having potential buyers travel to their offices, they brought their offices to them. At one stop, they parked the vehicle in Wal-Mart's parking lot. Everyone from the CEO to the VP of Finance came into the vehicle for a sales pitch and they walked away with an order that would make you fall out of your chair. Could you imagine how long it would take to get the entire executive team at Wal-Mart to come to your offices? But take your offices to them and watch the sales come pouring in. Believe me, if you are a B2B company, you need a mobile marketing program. If not, your competitors will have one soon ... and then who's laughing?"

POINTS TO REMEMBER

Experiential marketing is the wave of the PR future. In order to escape the information overload, the best way to connect with a target audience is to literally get in their face. Direct contact is always more effective, especially for product demonstrations, and the versatility of experiential marketing allows for the coordination and production of both general consumer and highly niche B2B campaigns.

But at the same time, be aware that experiential marketing requires far more planning and risk manage-

Experimental marketing is the wave of the PR future.

ment than traditional PR approaches. Having the right team in place, making sure that no potential liabilities can arise (remember the Boston debacle mentioned earlier in this chapter) and being able to respond to at-the-moment reactions are part of the game. Thus, extensive advance planning is needed before anyone hits the street.

A word on grassroots PR: yes! The best brand ambassador is the general public, so having public input in a PR campaign is a great idea ... provided that it is a transparent and honest effort. No one likes to be suckered into a scheme, and using grassroots PR to promote a hidden agenda (political, corporate or otherwise) will inevitably backfire if the scheme is revealed in all of its shameless ignoble failings. In that case, grassroots quickly turns to mud.

Where PR Fails (and It Doesn't Have To)

"If we did all the things we are capable of doing, we would literally astound ourselves."

—Thomas Edison

6

N ow it is time to talk about something that most PR professionals will prefer not to acknowledge: the shortcomings of the industry. Yes, even PR has its limits!

Actually, that's not entirely correct. It is not PR itself that is the cause of the problem. Rather, it is the PR practitioners who are their own worst enemies. In too many areas, the PR professional betrays an astonishing level of ignorance towards issues, situations and concerns that should be front and center on their agenda sheets.

This chapter runs the risk of being the least popular among many PR professionals. Though perhaps in airing some of the lethal (if not fatal) flaws of the industry, we can work to bring improvement where it is needed the most.

BANGING ON THE C-SUITE DOOR

For those unfamiliar with the expression, "C-Suite" is business slang for the exclusive gathering of chief officers within a corporation or organization. Some of these individuals literally have the word "chief" in their titles: Chief Executive Officer, Chief Operating Officer, Chief Financial Officer, Chief Information Officer.

Some entities (not many) also have a Chief Marketing Officer (CMO), under whose control the PR functions would operate. In the scheme of things, it is a relatively recent development: as far as anyone can determine, the very first person to be granted this title was Sergio Zyman, who was Chief Marketing Officer at the Coca-Cola Company from 1993 to 1998.

But within the C-Suite, the CMO is usually the weakest link in the executive chain. In November 2005, the CMO Council issued a report that exposed the problems in this C-Suite niche. The survey of 400 executives found only 10 percent believed their marketing groups were "highly influential and strategic" within the company. Furthermore, less than half expressed confidence that their efforts were "well regarded and respected."

"This study confirms marketers need to move from a tactical orientation to a more analytic and strategic approach that will enable them to realign marketing initiatives with the overall corporate mission," said Donovan Neale-May, executive director of the CMO Council, in a news release that accompanied the report.

Even more troubling is that CMOs rarely stay long in the C-Suite. A July 2004 survey from research firm Spencer Stuart found that the average tenure for chief marketing officers at the top 100 branded companies is just 23 months. In comparison, chief executive officers stay in the C-Suite, on average, 54 months.

The Spencer Stuart survey discovered that "14 percent of CMOs for the world's top brands have been with their companies for more than three years — and nearly half are new to the job over the last 12 months."

Now, the realm of CMO goes far beyond PR – it can encompass all aspects of marketing (including advertising, sales management, product development, market research, customer service and internal communications).

But that raises a question: where do PR professionals sit at the C-Suite table? The answer: they don't. Or at least they're not there yet.

We hear how PR should be at the table, but I would contend most PR people are not qualified to be at the table.
—**Terry Hemeyer**

"We hear how PR should be at the table, but I would contend most PR people are not qualified to be at the table," says Terry Hemeyer, senior counsel at Pierpont Communications in Houston and a senior lecturer on the faculty of the University of Texas at Austin. "First, they don't understand the business well enough. Second, they are too tactical – they are too worried about using the AP style in press releases and not about the company, its goals and its objectives."

And herein lies the problem. PR is proactive in its promotional aspects, but too often it is reactive when it comes to the bigger picture. Namely, when it comes to the bottom line issues affecting a company or organization's financial health, PR professionals are often clueless.

"The folks on mahogany row already nod reverently in the direction of lawyers and CPAs and other specialists," explains Richard Barger, president of Barger Consulting. "PR pros need to figure out what keeps the boss up at night and provide objective-based, business-oriented solutions. No CEO gives a rip

No CEO gives a rip about whether you use a fifth color on that brochure, but they sure care about reducing turnover, increasing sales, cutting costs, improving profits and many other business metrics.
—**Richard Barger**

about whether you use a fifth color on that brochure, but they sure care about reducing turnover, increasing sales, cutting costs, improving profits and many other business metrics."

Barger's advice for addressing this situation: "Become a businessperson who understands biz-com, not a communicator who is trying to communicate 'about' business."

J. Brooks Christol at Healthways echoes Barger's sentiments. "It is easy to blame the woes of our industry on the C-Suite, but the truth is that we are just as much to blame as anyone," he says. "So many people come into the industry thinking it is easy to garner press attention, that their role is to get a client in front of a reporter, do a follow-up to make sure the story runs and then move on to the next appearance. The problem is that we don't pay attention to the details and nuances that are constantly evolving, the details that can skew the tone of the messages we're sending out."

Speaking of sending out messages, there is also another problem that PR people don't seem cognizant about....

WORKING WITH (NOT AGAINST) THE MEDIA

My first job in PR (at a mid-sized agency in New York) came after I worked eight years as a journalist. When I was introduced to my agency colleagues, there was an air of astonishment: I was the first person in the company who actually worked as a journalist. I'm not joking when I state that these PR people looked at me with the same degree of bafflement that the 18th century zoologists must have conveyed upon seeing a platypus for the first time.

Perhaps this was an extreme situation on its own, but it provided an acute illustration of a very common problem within PR: the lack of knowledge about media people. Specifically, too many PR people have no idea how the media operates or what editors, journalists and news producers genuinely need from them. And this dilemma is not exclusive to the lowly account executives who are new to the field – too many heads of PR agencies and communications officers within major companies and nonprofits are equally ignorant of what the media needs from them.

For starters, news media people do not need to be reminded that you sent them a press release. As you may imagine, the average journalist receives anywhere from a dozen to several dozen press releases a day (the above-average journalist probably gets even more, since they've made the A-list of journalism and many PR people want to get their attention).

There is a right way and a wrong way to follow up on a press release. Most PR people, it seems, take the wrong way: by directly calling the journalist and asking: "Did you get the press release I sent you?" Very few journalists are endeared to that school of inquiry.

"Many journalists are overworked, and the last thing they want to do is get a call from some idiot trying to push something they have no interest in writing about," states Patrick Ogle of Facets, the Chicago-based DVD distributor. For Ogle, the inquiry is not so much the problem as its contents – particularly if the PR professional is pushing something unwanted or completely irrelevant to the editorial mission of the journalists' outlet.

"I remember a PR company trying to get serious journalists to write about guys who bowl in their underwear," adds Ogle. "After 100 of those calls you think all PR people are idiots."

Steve Ellis, senior vice president with Levick Strategic Communications in Washington, D.C., concurs. "Reporters look at many PR people negatively because many PR people do not understand what news is."

Reporters look at many PR people negatively because many PR people do not understand what news is.

—**Steve Ellis**

WORKING ON THE CHEAP

It is not uncommon for a PR endeavor to be underfinanced – either in-house or when it's outsourced to a third-party PR rep or agency.

However, this disadvantage can sometimes be turned into an advantage. Eric Phelps, executive director of the New Art Center in Newtonville, Mass., often handles the PR for his nonprofit arts center. This, however, is by default and not by design.

"Small nonprofits don't have the financial resources to afford good marketing materials which are often used to generate good PR," he says. "They may also not have the budget to treat critical people for lunch or at events, which helps to develop relationships and adds to the 'schmooze factor.' When a small nonprofit contacts a newspaper or other media outlet, we are typically among literally thousands of groups that submit information. The larger places can develop contacts, invite them to exciting and interesting events (sometimes with celebs) and therefore develop 'buzz' about their organization."

For Phelps, the lack of an in-house PR professional and the lack of funds to employ an outside expert is a problem. "Small groups rarely have a staff person devoted to PR," he continues. "If they do, it's a 'Development and Marketing' position, with

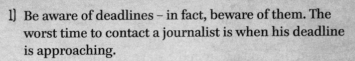

PHIL'S INSIDER PR TIP 7   How Not to Irritate Journalists

If you want to avoid making an enemy of the media, here are some basic tips you need to remember.

1) Be aware of deadlines – in fact, beware of them. The worst time to contact a journalist is when his deadline is approaching.

2) Be cognizant that most monthly publications are put together anywhere from two to four months in advance of publication. Weekly publications usually close on Fridays (sometimes Thursdays, but rarely earlier). Thus, if you want to hit either of these types of media outlets, get your news to them well before they are ready to go to the printer.

3) Daily publications often close late at night, so try to arrange your news pitch for early in the day.

4) For daily TV and radio news, be aware of when the main news programs air. If you want to get a story on the 6:00 news, don't call the news director at 5:30.

5) If you have any doubt concerning these tips, do yourself a favor: call the media people directly and ask them when their deadlines are. But be sure to call them earlier in the day … and not when they are actually on deadline!

the emphasis on the fundraising aspects of the job. If there is some money for the above, or even you have some creative ideas for implementing them, you may not have the time to devote to public relations beyond the necessary fundraising meetings. Singular 'publicity events' rarely happen and even getting people to attend your signature events can be difficult if you don't have time to send proper invites. Of all of the things on a nonprofit organization's 'To Do' list, PR often falls by the wayside – in fact, it most often does. Some groups have had success hiring a consultant or firm for one or two PR projects, to push forth a particular event or agenda."

Yet this situation doesn't have to degenerate into a negative experience. "Still, with some creativity and/or chutzpah you might find that you can spin the story of your group, your project or your mission to getting good media coverage," Phelps adds. "The interesting thing is that newspapers are often looking for something 'good' to write about, especially in the face of overwhelming bad news."

Here are a few tricks he's found useful:

♦ Send them great photos. Dance photos or really interesting art work has a better chance of getting you an article than anything you could possibly say.

♦ Send non-holiday items during the holidays. (Phelps got great press with color photos last year of an "I Shot Andy Warhol" screening, probably, he says, because the papers were sick of "Nutcracker" and "A Christmas Carol" press releases.)

♦ Tell a story. If there's something interesting about the piece of art, or about the person making it, try to pitch that.

IN THE EVENT OF CRISIS...

Crisis communications and crisis management should be the crowning achievement of the PR world – it shows the ability of the PR professional to take charge of a potentially explosive situation and effectively defuse it. And, indeed, there are many sterling examples of crisis communications efforts (the most notably being the 1982 Tylenol tampering crisis cited in Chapter Two).

But at the same time, too much crisis communications is reactive and not proactive. The PR person is often the last to know something has gone very wrong – and the reason for that is because of what was stated earlier about the lack of access to the C-Suite. In this case, it is a double-edged problem. For the PR professional, who is not considered an equal to the others at the C-Suite table, it means having to work overtime (literally and figuratively) to put out the fires created by a crisis. And for the executives in the C-Suite, who are unaware of what the PR professional can provide to their mission, it exposes them and a multitude of problems (ranging from tarnished images to criminal investigation and all points in between).

"PR professionals need to convince the C-Suite, especially the General Counsel, that they must understand that news is controversy and controversy is news," says Levick's Steve Ellis. "Crisis management to a large extent is news management. If you do not understand news, you cannot manage a crisis. To extrapolate: if a company, organization or country does not understand news, the people running these entities will fail. It's that simple."

Mike Paul, president of MGP & Associates in New York, believes that most corporations only consider reputation management as a reaction to a crisis, rather than as a proactive process to stave off

> *Truth, transparency, accountability, humility and consistency are the building blocks or reputation bricks for a corporation.*
> —**Mike Paul**

potential problems. "Indeed, crisis preparedness is not usually at the forefront of corporate communications planning," he says. "Ironically, it should be because more and more corporations are facing reputations in crisis because of unethical, immoral and legal behavior of executives within the corporate world. Just open your daily newspaper and count the dozens of stories highlighting corporate misdeeds."

Paul continues: "Truth, transparency, accountability, humility and consistency are the building blocks or reputation bricks for a corporation. A corporation is made up of many individuals. These rules are for executives, employees and support staff. They are easy to talk about, but difficult to consistently put into practice because of deceitful human behavior."

At the New York agency Peppercom, an in-house crisis communications program called CARES is used for crises in need of such assistance. The CARES acronym stands for **C**omposure and collection of information, **A**ssessment, **R**eaction, **E**valuation and **S**uccess (okay, we'll forgive them for stretching that "C" a bit).

"CARES has been effectively implemented for Peppercom clients of all sizes to create realistic and logical processes to follow during and after the onset of a crisis," explains Ted Birkhahn, managing director at Peppercom. "CARES also provides a true measuring stick by which these crisis management processes and actions can be continually improved after a crisis takes place, allowing for quick modification, if necessary."

Birkhahn points out that his agency delivers a three-part crisis training-drill-assessment program to prepare senior executives and crisis teams for any crisis situation. This includes a mock-crisis situation (which creates a two- to three-hour imaginary crisis scenario that is captured on videotape), which is then followed by a diagnostic review of that mock-crisis that results in a professional assessment and recommendation of where improvement may be needed.

"We carefully review the video, process, notes taken by the team, their assessment of how well they did and our own ongoing assessment," explains Birkahn. "This would showcase a gap that might exist on how well they think they are prepared but really aren't. Through our assessment, our deliverable is to present 'the good, bad and ugly' of how well the team did and to provide detailed recommendations (being consistent with client procedures) to the team the next day. These recommendations would actually be presented in a three-ring binder. Based upon the crisis team's actual handling of the simulated crisis, we will also present them with a fictitious end result that occurred (i.e., an article, directive from within the company, etc.), so they can truly understand how their actions led to something good, bad or nothing at all."

The day after that mock-crisis, Birkhahn and his team holds a strategic training session to review specific findings, offer recommendations and then offer training tips on how the crisis should be handled the next time around. That can last from three to four hours.

As you may gather, that level of in-depth crisis training requires time, energy and the full cooperation of senior management. For the PR professionals who can obtain all of that, the end result could be invaluable. For those who cannot, however ... well, let's just say it might be helpful to have a clean rag ready in the event the fan gets hit with you-know-what.

MEDIA TRAINING

Sometimes in the life of a company or an organization, the chief executive needs to go before the media. Not everyone is comfortable speaking in front of strangers, and even fewer people are comfortable under the glare of video camera lights. This is where media training comes in.

Or, to be precise, this is where media training should come in. When the PR officer doesn't have easy access to the chief executive, a serious problem can take root in the event the chief executive is needed to speak with the

Many PR professionals happily schedule interviews without worrying if the chief executive will make a good impression with the media – particularly if the interview is being videotaped. That is a huge mistake.

media. And it doesn't necessarily have to do with addressing a potential scandal or concern – even a relatively benign Q&A can be problematic if the chief executive isn't comfortable with the media.

Many PR professionals happily schedule interviews without worrying if the chief executive will make a good impression with the media – particularly if the interview is being video-taped. That is a huge mistake. Even the most self-confident chief executive could benefit from advice on framing answers, speaking clearly and presenting the best possible image.

"A CEO should have media training more often than once a year," suggests Mike Paul. "In fact, consistent weekly practice and role play with a seasoned communications consultant with excellent media relations experience is advised. The media prep should include difficult Q & A sessions, best and worst case scenario planning regarding potential questions and feed-back after the interview. The President of the United States is a good example. He is in the media daily, his ego doesn't allow him to say: 'I don't need any practice!' He understands the value to consistently prep for all interviews. I tell our clients: if this rule is good enough for the President of the United States, it should be good enough for a corporate CEO."

Ironically, not every government official is as confident in dealing with the media as Paul's perception of the Oval Office occupant. "So many people in government are so scared of the media," notes Brandi North-Williams, public information officer for the City of Charlotte (N.C.) Solid Waste Services. "And in their defense, the media is always looking for the government wrongdoing scandal. So, media training is extremely important in a government setting. Government officials must have a level of knowledge of media tricks and how to respond."

However, not everyone firmly embraces media training as the be-all/end-all. "Media training is essential and critical," says Suzanne O'Leary Lopez of Santa Fe's Thornburg Mortgage Home Loans. "But more importantly it needs to be teamed up with message training, and that combination is by far the most important element for a spokesperson's success in developing important relationships with the media and managing the company's reputation through articulate communication."

Jay Stuck is even more critical. "I used to think that media training was a waste of time, for the most part," he recalls. "An afternoon with a media trainer, even a good one, is not going to replace the heart attack-inducing experience of actually being in a live interview. Like anything else in life, practice makes perfect. You need to have lots of live interviews to truly be comfortable with doing them and one afternoon isn't going to help very much. I've found most of the corporate people forget much of what was covered anyway. But, (and here's where I may sound as if I'm changing my opinion) my sense is that today the public wants to see the head of the company talking about the troubles, not his PR person. They want to see the head of the oil company explaining why pricing is up; the head of the airline explaining why the plane went down. They surely don't want to see a polished PR person not necessarily answering the questions. So, I'm inclined to recommend the media training if the talking head has to be the head of the company. And hope that some of the good stuff sticks after a day-long session (if the head of the company is willing to even give you that much time)."

PHIL'S INSIDER PR TIP 8   Putting on the Right Look

One aspect of media training that is often overlooked is appearance. Sometimes it's accidental (PR professionals are so tied up with words that they forget imagery) and sometimes it is intentional (do you want to tell the boss he or she looks like a slob?).

But don't think that people (especially reporters) don't pick up on a sloppy appearance. I once represented a grooming expert who had a dandruff problem. Needless to say, a callous reporter for a national news syndicate made a catty reference to my client's flaky problem and it created serious ill-will with the badly insulted client.

Therefore, it is crucial that any media training focus pay very, very close attention to questions of looking good. Here are some tips provided by Ellen York, the nationally recognized consultant and president of the Ellen York Image Institute (visit her online at www.ellenyork.com). This is the advice that York gives to men and women who are going to represent their companies and organizations before the public and the cameras:

- **HAIRSTYLE.** Men need to have an updated hairstyle, just like women. It may be time to visit a new stylist for a current style and color that will flatter your appearance and create a more professional look.

- **FACIAL HAIR.** This look can be distracting if you have a face full of hair. Ask your stylist to trim your beard, mustache and sideburns to allow people to see who they're talking to.

- **PERFUME/COLOGNE.** Everyone wants to smell good, but no one wants to be so overpowering that they offend everyone else. A daily application of deodorant should suffice but if you want to wear perfume, a small dab at the wrists and neck will be enough. You never know – a potential client may be allergic to strong scents and be "repelled" if you wear too much fragrance.

◆ **NAILS.** Beautiful, polished nails can be a wonderful complement to a professional look. However, nails that are too long, painted in a bright (or too dark) color, or even those that are natural but unkempt, can be distracting. Men should also pay close attention to their nails and keep them short and clean. Women and men alike can benefit from a manicure. You can't imagine how many people notice a set of well-kept hands!

◆ **FINGERS AND HANDS.** Watch yourself for other behaviors, such as a tapping your fingers or pen, biting your nails, playing with your hair or crossing your arms when you are nervous. These habits can be distracting to a client, which can cause him or her to lose interest in what you're saying.

◆ **VOICE, PART ONE.** Check your voice. Listen to a voice-mail message that you've recorded. If it's nasal or too low or too soft, you may want to seek a professional voice coach or someone who can help address the issue.

◆ **VOICE, PART TWO.** Many people talk too fast when they're anxious or tense. The next time you are in a stressful situation, such as a meeting with a potential client, listen to your own voice. Practice talking slower and fully enunciating the words.

◆ **TEETH.** Remember to a smile! People love to see a happy person.

CSR IRRELEVANCIES

Now it's time to set off a few firecrackers: PR (at least from the business world) fails when it forces too much attention on corporate social responsibility (or CSR for those who prefer acronyms to English).

CSR is the catch-phrase that encompasses the notion of what Oz's Wizard referred to as "good-deed doing," in which the corporate world shows it has a heart and a conscience by getting involved in a variety of socially relevant activities such as volunteerism, philanthropy, sponsorship of nonprofits and so forth. On the agency side, this might involve taking on pro bono accounts (usually involving smaller nonprofits) with the plan of using PR connections to raise awareness of some socially, culturally or even spiritually relevant cause.

On the surface, it seems like a wonderful idea. But from a PR standpoint, CSR has become an inane distraction which ultimately never serves its purpose because it is grounded in a basic flaw: calling attention away from the corporation's mission with fluffy news and self-congratulatory accolades concerning isolated actions of good citizenship.

Reality check: CSR is a defense mechanism that gets set up when a corporation and/or its leaders begin to generate seriously rotten PR. Of course, responsible corporations don't need to blow their own horns on how great they are because anyone operating in an ethical and moral manner already has the respect of their customers and investors.

> *Responsible corporations don't need to blow their own horns on how great they are because anyone operating in an ethical and moral manner already has the respect of their customers and investors.*

Consider, as an example, the case of Ford Motor Company, which issued a glowing press release in late 2006 noting it had been "rated among the top 25 companies in the world in corporate social responsibility reporting by 'Tomorrow's Value: The Global Reporters.' Ford is the only automaker among the top 25 of the 50 companies demonstrating best practices in corporate social responsibility."

"Tomorrow's Value" is a corporate sustainability report developed by the combined efforts of the United Nations Environment Program, Standard & Poor's and SustainAbility Ltd. Ford was honored for being "the first in the automotive industry to develop, implement and report a Code of Basic Working Conditions."

Ironically, that press release was distributed around the same time when Autoblog reported that "Ford is looking to rid itself of 10,000 of its 38,500 salaried workers by 2008" by using buyouts or involuntary layoffs.

Really, is there a point in having a Code of Basic Working Conditions if tens of thousands of people are being cut from their jobs? Where's the social responsibility when mass layoffs have damaging effects on the regional economies that relied on the company's presence as an employer, especially in Michigan?

A few companies have always operated by trumpeting how wonderful they are in regard to social responsibility – Ben & Jerry's and The Body Shop were ubiquitous (and, ultimately, emetic) in reminding us what good citizens they were. Ultimately, such PR shenanigans didn't help their respective bottom lines.

From the C-Suite perspective, CSR is bad for business because it diverts time, energy and resources from more important functions. Betsy Atkins, CEO of Baja Ventures, a venture capital firm concentrating on technology and life sciences, was perhaps the most eloquent in her summary of the fallacy of CSR in an essay from the Nov. 28, 2006 edition of Forbes magazine:

"The concept of corporate social responsibility deserves to be challenged. It seems that political correctness has obfuscated the important business points. It is absolutely correct to expect that corporations should be 'responsible' by creating quality products and marketing them in an ethical manner, in compliance with laws and regulations and with financials represented in an honest, transparent way to shareholders. However, the notion that the corporation should apply its assets for social purposes, rather than for the profit of its owners, the shareholders, is irresponsible.

The corporation's goal is to act on behalf of its owners. The company's owners – its shareholders – can certainly donate their own assets to charities that promote causes they believe in. They can buy hybrid cars to cut back on fossil fuel consumption or support organizations that train the hard-core unemployed. But it would be irresponsible for the management and directors of a company, whose stock these investors purchased, to deploy corporate assets for social causes."

Where PR people should be active in regard to CSR is the exact place where they are often absent: in the Investor Relations side of things. Sister Patricia Wolf, executive director of the Interfaith Center for Corporate Responsibility (an international coalition of 275 faith-based institutional investors) told me that she never deals with PR people whenever there is an issue of curious corporate activities – she goes straight to the CEOs. The absence of PR professionals from the Investor Relations ranks (particularly in targeting the growing socially responsible investing sector) would suggest that too many PR people have no clue how to approach CSR.

CSR, from an American PR perspective, has become an irritating distraction that is so overpowering that some companies even devote resources to creating special reports detailing just what wonderful corporate citizens they are. That kind of nonsense doesn't fool anyone – particularly the socially responsible institutional investors who are more interested in deeply ingrained problems of corporate malfeasance and dubious business practices (especially in distant countries where companies or their subcontractors exploit the local working classes).

And that's where CSR fails miserably in most cases: it becomes so obsessed with highlighting happy news (no matter how trivial) that it gets caught off-guard when socially responsible investors start agitating for change. That sector has $2.3 trillion in capital to invest and they don't give a damn about touchy-feely publicity stunts. More often than not, PR officers wind up doing crisis control when the socially responsible investors want to see genuine examples of CSR and not the PR puffery.

If a company wants to get involved in some benevolent activity, like a walkathon or a mentoring program, there's nothing wrong with that. Nor is there anything wrong with an isolated press release highlighting this activity. But getting carried away with an excessive PR campaign trumpeting foolish CSR is as valueless as the golden calf worshipped by our Biblical brethren – who, as punishment for genuflecting to the wrong deity, wound up in pretty bad shape.

POINTS TO REMEMBER

PR is not a panacea. It is part of an overall marketing strategy, but it should not be misidentified (intentionally or otherwise) as the be-all/end-all approach to marketing.

PR should be proactive, not reactive. Even in the response to a crisis, the strategy should be one of getting ahead of the story and not being held hostage to it.

PR will not work if the PR professional is unaware of the basic goals, operations and personality of the company or organization being represented. This happens

> *PR should be proactive, not reactive. Even in the response to a crisis, the strategy should be one of getting ahead of the story and not being held hostage to it.*

frequently when agencies are hired for the PR function – the PR reps are outsiders, both literally and figuratively. But this also occurs when there is an in-house PR expert (hence our earlier citation of the frustration at not being part of the celebrated C-Suite gatherings). When the PR professional is the last to know what's going on, it usually bodes ill for all parties.

Go Forth Into the PR World

*"Strategy without tactics is the slowest route to victory.
Tactics without strategy is the noise before defeat."*

—Sun Tzu

7

So where do we go from here? The flippant answer would be: on to another book, as this is our last chapter. But the serious answer is this: PR requires an open mind and endless talent for communications, planning and patience. It is not a field for the weak or the stupid (though, sadly, more than a few of them have found their way into it).

Today's PR requires a professional code for new practitioners and seasoned pros to live by. Because no one has bothered to present a professional code to meet the evolving state of the industry, allow me to fill the void.

AVOID THE FIVE BOO-BOOS THAT WRECK PR CAMPAIGNS

In my ongoing work as the editor of a mortgage banking publication, I receive a daily bombardment of press releases concerning a wide variety of issues, events and products. One might assume that these press releases are exclusive to the mortgage banking industry – after all, that's the subject my magazine covers.

So imagine my surprise when I opened an e-mail from a PR agency and found the following text:

```
<<< DENVER, Jan. 23, 2007 -- What's a good way
to put today's shopper to sleep? Pack your store
with dull displays and monotonous merchandising
techniques. Before you know it, they'll be
catching zzz's in a quiet corner of the store!

Wooly Bully Wear(TM) (http://www.woolybullywear.
com), a Denver-based company that specializes
in women's fleece outerwear, knows the secret to
keeping shoppers awake and alert to fabulous
fashion - strategic merchandising techniques
and dazzling displays. In response, Wooly
Bully Wear(TM) is now designed with "fresh-
look" merchandising for more practical, dynamic
presentation. >>>
```

Can you see the connection between mortgage banking and Wooly Bully Wear? How in the world a publicist for a women's clothing line could imagine that this product would be featured (prominently or otherwise) in a mortgage banking publication is beyond me.

This is not a question of spam, mind you. Rather, it is a case of a PR professional acting like a PR amateur: just throw press releases willy-nilly to the winds and hope they wind up in the right places.

Which leads me to my concern about attention to detail or the lack thereof. A good way to screw up a PR campaign is to make five simple errors that could easily be avoided if one pays attention to doing the basic job correctly. In the proverbial nutshell, here are the five boo-boos that will turn a champ into a chump:

1) **MEDIA LISTS THAT ARE WILDLY INCORRECT.** Our friends at Wooly Bully Wear (who, in fairness, have a very nice product line) learned that the harsh way. But in all seriousness, this is the easiest mistake to avoid.

Building and maintaining an up-to-date media list is PR 101. It is not difficult to determine which person at what media outlet is going to receive press releases. It is a good idea to update the list at least three times a year, given that the media industry has an uncommonly high turnover rate and last week's editorial contact might have skedaddled to a better-paying opportunity elsewhere. Thus, do an easy fact check to make sure everyone on the list is still at their job. (I am reminded by a real dum-dum PR person who proudly showed me a media mailing list that included 15 people who were no longer employed at the companies on the list, plus one who passed away three years earlier!)

2) **PR COPY THAT IS FULL OF MISTAKES.** Remember that your material is going to people who make a living by writing and editing. The average Joe may not think

> *The average Joe may not think twice about a typo, mixed metaphor or dangling participle, but the editorial contact won't be very impressed to find press releases and pitch letters full of mistakes.*

twice about a typo, mixed metaphor or dangling participle, but the editorial contact won't be very impressed to find press releases and pitch letters full of mistakes. And that also extends to web site text. A certain PR industry trade publication (which will not be identified here) recently launched an online competition designed to honor remarkable achievements within the profession. That's perfectly noble, but there's little nobility in the promotional text for that competition – which is quoted here in its original, uncorrected version.

"On the home page of (publication name), we we profile PR professionals who've had a PR-related win, achievement or newsworthy event. We're giving you bragging rights to share with the PR community a major success and connect you with new friends in the business."

Oh dear, two sentences and two big boo-boos. I like the "we we" in the first sentence (what does that call for, a copy editor or a diuretic?). And that run-on of a second sentence? Enough said. Always have an extra set of eyes proofread everything before it goes into the world.

3) **LACK OF PROPER CONTACT INFORMATION.** This should go without saying, but it needs to be said: all PR materials need to have full contact data. This includes the telephone numbers and email addresses of the individuals listed as the media liaisons. It is astonishing how many press releases are sent out without liaison contacts (especially for press releases posted in online newsrooms – I've spent too much time clicking around online newsrooms in search of the person who supposedly is going to provide media input). If a press announcement is related to a specific company, have the company's contact data (address, phone number, URL) as part of the press release. Since paper-based press releases gave way to emailed releases, too many PR people forget to include the full contact data of the companies being promoted. This is especially problematic for our friends in the business-to-business trade media, who frequently include company phone numbers as part of their coverage.

4) **NOT HAVING PHOTOGRAPHS, OR HAVING LOUSY QUALITY SHOTS.** This is especially a bother when it comes to promoting new products, upcoming entertainment productions or bylined articles credited to corporate executives. As a journalist, I've been flummoxed for years by PR people who either don't have photographs

to go with whatever they're promoting or who provide the crummiest low-res photos imaginable. (Word of advice: all digital pictures should be 300 dpi or higher – and if you don't know what that means, then you are really in trouble!)

Word of advice: all digital pictures should be 300 dpi or higher – and if you don't know what that means, then you are really in trouble!

5) **ASKING THE ONE QUESTION THAT MEDIA PEOPLE HATE MOST OF ALL.** The question: "Did you get the press release I sent you?" There is not a single media professional in the world that wants to have their daily routine interrupted by a PR person tapping around to get an answer about the status of a press release. Why? Now imagine if your local utility called you to inquire: "Did you get the electric bill we sent?" Or if your favorite department store called you to ask: "Did you get the new catalog we mailed the other week?" Or if your bank called to find out: "Did you get the monthly statement we sent you the other day?" Kind of silly, yes? So how do you think a media person feels if they get a call from a PR person asking for the specific status of a press release that was forwarded to them anywhere from one hour to three weeks previously? The answer: there are ways to get the media's attention without asking that toxic question.

IF YOU WON'T GO THE FULL MILE, GET OFF THE ROAD

I used to know the head of a PR agency (we'll call him Mr. Rip-off and you'll know why momentarily) and he once found himself in a very unusual situation. One of his clients, a second-tier security consulting firm, abruptly began to bubble up with a dramatic amount of activity. All of the hubbub was due to a security consultant who discovered that he loved to be the center of media attention. This consultant, who specialized in speaking on issues relating to the post-9/11 environment, became fairly ubiquitous in a short time thanks to interviews published in major newspapers and guest shots on national talk shows.

And how do you think Mr. Rip-off reacted to this? By praising his team for energizing this sleepy account (which went from two hits a month to seven hits a week)? By reminding his client on the value of a well-focused PR effort? No, Mr. Rip-off literally slammed on the brakes, ordering his account personnel to stop pushing that consultant's media profile. From what I was told, Mr. Rip-off's exact words were "I'm not being paid enough to justify that level of activity."

Huh? Considering that Mr. Rip-off's account team did their aggressive work primarily by email contact and an occasional phone call, there was no excess financial output to generate A-list media coverage. But that wasn't the case. In Mr. Rip-off's mind, he was being paid "X" amount for a monthly retainer and the client wasn't deserving of more than a certain level of media hits. Of course, that wasn't in the client's contract.

I'll say it again: Huh? But I'm actually feigning surprise, because Mr. Rip-off's actions are not an aberration. One of the dirtier secrets of the agency side of PR involves the slamming of breaks on active smaller accounts. For years, I've heard stories of smaller companies who hired PR agencies and wondered why they weren't getting very good media coverage. And, truth be told, I've witnessed it repeatedly on a firsthand basis.

Why does this happen? The answer is simple but troubling: the agencies are more obsessed with milking their cash cow accounts, and the smaller companies (with their smaller monthly fees) are literally designated to afterthought status.

Here's another real-life anecdote. My pal Matt is the head of marketing for a software company that serves a very specific business niche. The company isn't tiny, but it would be an exaggeration to call it mid-sized. Anyway, they hired a major Manhattan PR firm (no names here, we're all friends) to promote them. But after a few months, Matt was bothered by the lack of quality coverage. There were a couple of new product briefs here and a personnel announcement or two there, but the level of media coverage his company needed was suspiciously absent.

So Matt called the PR reps and he was told, rather bluntly, that the publications he wanted to appear in were just not interested in that story. Matt then called the publications himself, and discovered something rather interesting: not only were the publications highly interested, but they also were never contacted by that major Manhattan PR firm.

In the scheme of things, Matt's PR firm had some of the world's largest corporations as clients and they saw his company as small potatoes. The large accounts held the bulk of their attention and, not surprisingly, had media coverage to spare.

Oh, I should say "Matt's ex-PR firm" – he fired them when he got air of their tricks. The same thing happened with Mr. Rip-off: his client dropped him when they learned why the media spigot was abruptly turned off on their interview-happy consultant.

Many PR agencies avoid representing smaller companies strictly because of fees (they literally feel it's not worth the bother). For those who deign to accept these companies as clients, they inevitably delegate these accounts to junior level account staff with the expectation that nothing significant should come about. The smaller companies, who often don't know better (if they did, they'd do their own PR) usually accept the story of a lack of media interest for a while. But when the costs of a monthly PR retainer outweigh the promised benefits of representation, they pull out with bitterness over not getting what they paid for.

Honest and talented PR people go the extra mile for their clients, while the Mr. Rip-offs of the industry can't even be bothered to go the contractually required distance. Sadly, it is the Mr.

> *Honest and talented PR people go the extra mile for their clients, while the Mr. Rip-offs of the industry can't even be bothered to go the contractually required distance.*

Rip-offs who ruin things for the industry, as a lot of companies who get burned by such con artists junk the PR push altogether in favor of other marketing pursuits. In that scenario, the PR industry gets burned with a nasty image – and Mr. Rip-off and his ilk, who get lousy reputations and begin to lose business, will ultimately not be laughing all the way to the bank.

IF YOU ARE BLOCKED BY TRADITIONAL RULES OF ENGAGEMENT, DON'T BREAK THE RULES – DEMOLISH THEM

One of the main problems with PR is too many practitioners insist on following tried-and-true procedures. More often than not, that line of strategy produces desultory payback. But going above and beyond the proverbial call of duty will offer a greater chance to get your message heard – and a greater return on investment, too.

Case in point: Hewlett-Packard's Digital Publishing Solutions needed to spread the word on its commercial printing presses, but reaching their target of small- to medium-sized printing enterprise customers, graphic design agencies and paper manufacturers was a challenge. In the ideal world, these customers would come to HP to test the machines. But not everyone could take the time to leave their offices to visit HP.

The solution: HP came to them. The company launched its Impressions Road Show in late 2002 with the goal of visiting every possible customer for its industrial-sized printing presses (no mean feat, as these machines weighed about 10,000 pounds). The machines were mounted inside a truck that criss-crossed the country, making stops in parking lots and trade shows. In the first year alone, the tour accommodated repre-sentatives from 2,600 companies, who participated in hands-on product demos and booked $140 million in sales.

The tour was also honored with an Ex Award from *Event Marketing Magazine*. Yvon Russell, president of Aspen Marketing Services (which coordinated the tour on behalf of Hewlett-Packard), accepted the Ex Award and told *Event Marketing Magazine*: "This has generated a higher degree of ROI than anything I have ever seen."

REMEMBER THAT PR IS A BUSINESS PRACTICE – ALWAYS THINK LIKE A BUSINESS PROFESSIONAL

PR involves a lot of written and oral communications. But ultimately, it is not a "writing gig." It is a business practice and people who plan to make a living in this industry need to think, act and behave like business professionals.

"I believe that PR professionals are business counselors," says Brandi North-Willams of Charlotte's Solid Waste Services. "It is our job to make sure that the image of the organiza-tion stays intact with internal and external audiences, while protecting the interests of everyone (and yes, I truly believe that as a PR practitioner we can honor the best interests of the company and all their constituents). To do that we are often dabbling in all parts of the business and helping each side of the table come to compromises ... we should get automatic Nobel Peace Prizes! So, as a definition: a *business management function* that creates mutually beneficial relationships between two parties for the goodwill of everyone."

KNOW WHAT PR CAN AND CANNOT DO FOR YOU – AND RECOGNIZE WHAT YOU CAN OR CANNOT ACHIEVE ON YOUR OWN

For Adam Dooley, vice president of marketing and communications at Cambrian Credit Union in Winnipeg, Manitoba, PR is a critical tool in a marketing strategy. However, he feels too many people have an incorrect assumption of what it can achieve.

"I believe some people approach public relations in general and media relations in particular with unrealistic expectations," he says. "They expect to see a glowing writeup on their credit union featured on the front page of their local paper. The reality is that it takes time to establish relationships with reporters, columnists and editors. You and your company need to demonstrate consistency and reliability to the media. Over time, we've found that key journalists come to call on us regularly for their stories, but that did not happen overnight."

For Dooley, the key to successful media coverage is a healthy relationship with the editors, reporters and producers who would be responsible for relaying the credit union's stories to their audiences.

> *I believe some people approach public relations in general and media relations in particular with unrealistic expectations.*
> —**Adam Dooley**

"We communicate our successes and noteworthy achievements to media, targeting specific media outlets and individual journalists who we know will be interested in our news," he says. "We're consistent, reliable and trustworthy. We work to cultivate good working relationships with key journalists. These tend to be journalists with specific interests in personal finance, technology or local corporate news. We use a national wire service to distribute some of our news releases, and we post our news releases on our public web site as well to ensure the information is there for journalists, our members and the general public."

Dooley's credit union handles its PR and marketing functions in-house, and he is satisfied with the control he has over this work. "We have the skills inside our organization to look after most of our public relations needs," he states. "We believe in an integrated marketing and communications model. Our public relations programs, our employee and member communications and our marketing all need to carry consistent messages. Handling our PR internally gives us a great deal of control over how we are positioned in our marketplace. It also helps us get important messages into the market quickly when we need to."

STAY ABREAST OF THE NEWS OF THE DAY

This might seem like common sense, but you'd be surprised how many self-described PR professionals are woefully unaware of what's happening in the world. Being out of the proverbial loop can stifle your creativity – particularly if you are using a current event or upcoming happening as the foundation of your PR outreach.

Take a tip from Steve Ellis, at Levick Strategic Public Relations, when it comes to staying on top of the world's news. "I try to keep up with the PR trades, but I get more ideas from *The Wall Street Journal*, *The Financial Times*, *The Economist* and other mainstream news media that offer global perspectives on all aspects of the conflicts that make up the news in the internationalized business, cultural and economic environment where we all live and must communicate," he says.

RECOGNIZE THAT NOT EVERYONE WILL APPRECIATE YOUR WORK

Of course, not every PR outreach is rewarded with glowing coverage. Sometimes there's a grouch in the pack who will spoil the fun with a putdown or worse.

For someone offering a new product, service or creative production, the worst PR would be a bad review. Berkeley, Calif.-based filmmaker Antero Alli encountered a seriously bad review in 1995 when his underground sci-film movie "The Drivetime" received an uncommonly harsh critique from the popular online magazine *Amazing World of Cult Movies*, which called the film a "silly mess" and dubbed Alli a "ninny." How did Alli respond to such harsh coverage? How do you react to harsh criticism, from both an artistic and an emotional standpoint?

"Though I often remind myself that any review is only one person's opinion, harsh reviews always hurt," says Alli. "What are you going to do? Stop reading all your reviews? That's just more self-stabbing victim bullshit. Why not pick up some objectivity and identify the bias of the reviewer just to see where they are coming from? Just for fun. When I do this, it's understandable why the *Amazing World of Cult Movies* calls me a 'ninny' and my movie a 'silly mess.' That's very funny. If I were as cynical and jaded as them, I'd probably say the same thing. To confound things, 'The Drivetime' was also given glowing reviews by *Wired Magazine*, the Pacific Film Archive and the NW Film Forum and these

> *Don't get into a pissing contest with the media over how they cover your PR outreach – you'll never win and only make yourself look silly in the process.*

guys didn't even call me names. Of course, their bias and outlook are, for the better part, already more aligned with my own. And I like that. If they had trashed my movie, I'd probably feel more hurt than the cynic who called me a ninny."

In short: you can't please everyone, so don't get pissed off if your PR outreach is not appreciated. And don't get into a pissing contest with the media over how they cover your PR outreach – you'll never win and only make yourself look silly in the process.

DON'T WASTE YOUR TIME WITH PR INDUSTRY AWARDS

My colleagues in the industry will hate me for this, but it needs to be stated without any degree of moderation: the PR industry awards are a waste of time and money and should be avoided.

Now, I am not stating this because my vines have cultivated a bumper crop of sour grapes. I've participated successfully in these competitions and my work snagged a few trophies. I've also had the responsibility (not privilege) of judging a few awards competitions. Having received PR awards and having determined which folks should receive them, I cannot help but feel they are of no value.

The reason for this negativity is twofold. First, there is an egregious glut of awards being handed out. The PR industry rivals the entertainment world for the mass quantity of honors it bestows on itself. Many of the national trade groups have annual awards, and the regional chapters of these groups have their own local awards. Likewise, many of the trade media have their own award competitions (though truth be told, those awards exist primarily as a major revenue enhancement scheme for the publishers – they can make some fast bucks on the entry fees – rather than as a genuinely sincere celebration of PR excellence).

Even within the individual award competitions, there are an absurdly high number of categories for the trophy chase. The PRSA's Silver Anvils, arguably the most respected of the industry's honors, has 16 different categories. Within each category are anywhere from two-to-six subcategories. For example, the Marketing Consumer Products Award has individual prizes going for best achievement in the Healthcare, Technology, Food & Beverage, Packaged Goods, Non-Packaged Goods and "Other" industries (the latter is a lump-'em-together of "categories not elsewhere defined," according to the PRSA).

But that's just the Silver Anvils – the Bronze Anvils have 50 different categories and subcategories. What's the difference in the awards? Well, according to the PRSA's web site, the "Silver Anvil Awards recognize complete programs incorporating sound research, planning, execution and evaluation" while the Bronze Anvil Awards "recognize outstanding public relations tactics, the individual items or components of programs."

The second problem is something that few award givers in the PR universe are willing to acknowledge: none of these awards competitions carry any clout beyond their respective organizing committees. Outside of the industry, PR awards are meaningless to the point of being thoroughly ignored. One individual responsible for an annual PR award presentation (who will not be identified here) used to boast fantastically that judging that particular award competition was "an honor." Strangely, that person had a bitch of a time trying to get anyone from the industry to embrace that "honor" and the judging was mostly done in-house.

I've done a search of national media and I have yet to locate a single news story about the results of a PR industry award.

The only genuine mainstream media coverage I could locate on a PR industry award presentation came from the weekly (and relatively unimportant) *New York Observer* on March 13, 2006, when it covered the PR Week Awards with the decidedly unflattering headline "Publicists Lauded for Flackery; PR Gods Get Freedom From Press" (the rest of the article was equally snarky).

Even if you bring the awards directly to the gathering point of the major national media, they won't pay attention. *PR News*, for example, hosts several of its awards (it has five different award competitions) at the National Press Club in Washington, D.C. – yet, to date, none of their awards ever received any national press coverage.

PR News, for example, hosts several of its awards (it has five different award competitions) at the National Press Club in Washington, D.C. – yet, to date, none of their awards ever received any national press coverage.

And that's just for the awards. There are also at least four different groups in the industry offering their own PR Hall of Fame. No further comment required on that!

LEARN TO TAKE YOUR HANDS OFF THE STEERING WHEEL

During the research phase of this book, I made an effort to reach out to as many creative and innovative people I could locate for case studies, commentaries and observations. Nearly everyone I contacted was very happy to donate their time and wisdom for this offering.

But there was one considerable exception: a financial services company that specializes in loans and investment products to U.S. military personnel. I received a copy of a very clever case study from that company about how they orchestrated a

successful readership survey for their internal quarterly magazine. It was impressive and it would've been perfect for this
book. But you won't find it here because their PR person was
a control freak.

My communications with this PR person began in a rather
benign manner: I sent her an email asking whether I could cite
her company's case study in the book and if I could send a few
questions her way to clarify aspects of the case study.

The PR person responded: "Our CMO has asked if our
company name will be published with the case study and also if
we'll have final approval rights before this is printed?"

Obviously, this is a curious response. Why would I publish an
in-depth case study and not mention the company's name?
Also, why would they need "final approval rights"? I asked
after that last point and received this response: "We're just
wondering if we would be able to see what is being written
before it is published."

As a writer, I normally do not allow the people I am interviewing to see articles before they are published. However, in
this case I didn't see any harm in letting the PR person see the
coverage I was planning. I informed the PR person that the
CMO could see the article before it is submitted for publication – but I intentionally stopped short of giving that CMO the
final sign-off on what was written.

The PR person clearly sensed there was something missing
in my okay, because then I received this message: "I have
confirmed that if we can have a signed agreement that
says we'll be able to approve the final content before being
published and that our company name will be published with
the case study, you may use our case study in your book."

Now this is a bit unprecedented – a smallish financial services provider demanding a "signed agreement" saying they can "approve the final content before being published"?

Guess what? The company's case study is not in the book. And simply because I am a nice guy, the company and its ridiculous PR person (and equally inane CMO) are not being identified by name.

This doesn't happen too often, but when it does it is frustrating: PR professionals who don't know when to take their hands off the proverbial steering wheel and allow other qualified professionals to drive the story. I can understand the concern about being misquoted in print (I've been there myself). But making blatant demands to control editorial content should not be the goal of a PR professional (or, in this case, a genuine PR amateur).

This should go without saying, but I will say it: if you are not comfortable having your company or executives involved in a particular forum, politely decline. Do not demand to have total control of editorial contents – journalists don't take that seriously and you'll lose what could easily have been wonderful coverage. In this situation, the company's case study didn't wind up in print – it wound up in the garbage can.

POINTS TO REMEMBER

What can damage the PR profession?

To answer that fatalistic inquiry, let's give the final expert opinion to Steve Cody of Peppercom.

1) The rise of the corporate procurement manager who tends to view PR as a commodity and seeks the low-cost provider. This depreciates the strategic nature of our service offering and, if left unchecked, could dramatically marginalize industry profits.

2) The lack of diversity in our workforce. This has been a big problem for years, but continues to receive little more than lip service. It's my belief that, until clients start forcing agencies to become more diverse, we won't. The bigger picture, longer range threat is that corporations will eventually only hire those firms whose workforce reflects and understands the diverse population they themselves are trying to reach.

3) The continuing misunderstanding of PR by the general public. I'd call this the Lizzie Grubman phenomenon, but it extends far beyond Grubman. Bottom line: as a result of Hollywood's portrayal of PR, most of us are perceived as either low-end party planners or sleazy corporate hacks willing to do or say anything.

4) Owning the digital communications opportunity. The seismic changes we've seen wrought by 'Web 2.0' present huge opportunities for the PR profession because we, arguably, have a better grasp on how to engage in open, honest discussions with consumers than do our advertising brethren. That said, very few PR firms are embracing the opportunities inherent in Web 2.0 or including Web 2.0 tactics in their strategic client planning. If we don't become more aggressive, some other service will fill the void.

Still, don't count PR out. After all, Microsoft founder Bill Gates is on record as saying: "If I was down to my last dollar, I'd spend it on public relations."

All things considered, it would be money well spent.

P hil Hall is one of the most provocative and vibrant figures in today's public relations and media industries. In his work as a PR executive, Hall received national attention as the president of Open City Communications, a public relations agency specializing in the promotion of small and mid-sized businesses. He was quoted on contemporary PR issues in the *Wall Street Journal* and *New York Times*, and he was profiled in *Entrepreneur* and *Business Start-Ups Magazine* for his innovative approaches to running an independent PR agency.

As a journalist, Hall was editor of *PR News*, a weekly trade journal. During this tenure, he was a popular speaker at PR industry functions and contributed a weekly commentary to the Net radio program "Stars of PR." He currently writes the provocative weekly column "The PR Gospel According to Phil" for Strumpette, an online resource covering PR trends and issues.

Apart from his work in PR, Hall is also well known for his film journalism. He is a contributing editor for the online magazine *Film Threat* and has written about cinema for the *New York Times*, *Wired Magazine* and *American Movie Classics Magazine*. He is the author of two film-related books: *The Encyclopedia of Underground Movies* and *Independent Film Distribution* (both published by Michael Wiese Productions).

Hall is also well known as a book critic. His book review column for the *New York Resident* weekly newspaper was nominated for a Pulitzer Prize in 2006, and he has written book reviews for *Publishers Weekly*, *Kirkus Reviews*, *EDGE Boston*, *Organica Quarterly* and NYCPOETRY.COM.

Additionally, he has written extensively on technology, business, history and social sciences. His writing has appeared in the *Hartford Courant*, *Delaware Today*, *New Architect* and *Nation's Business*. He also worked as a United Nations radio correspondent for Fairchild Broadcast News.

In September 2006, he became editor of *Secondary Marketing Executive*, a monthly magazine covering the mortgage banking industry. A veteran of financial services journalism, he was previously on the editorial team at the *ABA Banking Journal* and wrote the marketing column for *Credit Union News*.

Born in the Bronx, N.Y., Hall received a B.A. in journalism from Pace University. He lives in Connecticut.